Visa 1

Students Book

A two-year French course leading to the
General Certificate of Secondary Education

Tony Whelpton
Chief Examiner in French, The Associated Examining Board
Chief Examiner in French, The Southern Examining Group

Daphne Jenkins
Assistant French Teacher, Pate's Grammar School, Cheltenham
Senior Assistant Examiner, The Associated Examining Board
Reviser in French, The Southern Examining Group

LONGMAN GROUP UK LIMITED
Longman House
Burnt Mill, Harlow, Essex, CM20 2JE, England
and Associated Companies throughout the world

First published 1987

ISBN 0 582 22467 5

Set in 10/12 Linotron Aster

Printed in Great Britain by
Scotprint Limited, Musselburgh, Scotland

We are grateful to the following for permission to reproduce
photographs;
L'Office de Tourisme d'Angers, page 136; Service Documentation Ville
de Boulogne-sur-Mer, page 120; Camera Press, pages 117 below (photo
Ken Lambert) and 162 (photo David and Kate Urry); Documentation
Française, pages 87 (photos P. Bouvier) and 158 (photo SIRP PTT);
Keith Gibson, pages 16, 22 and 31 left; NAT Holidays, page 117 above;
Rapho, pages 119 (photo Serrallier), 153 above (photo Rémi Berli) and
153 below (photo J. Pavlovsky); SIC PTT, page 156; Topham, pages 31
right and 187.

Cover photograph by Brendan Hearne

Illustrated by Jean de Lemos.

Contents

To the pupil

In this book you are going to learn how to handle the different kinds of task that will face you when you come to take your GCSE examination. The examination is divided into four parts, each testing a different skill, as follows:

(a) Listening Comprehension – which tests how well you can understand French when you hear it spoken;

(b) Reading Comprehension – which tests how well you can understand French when you see it written down;

(c) Speaking – which tests how well you are able to make yourself understood when you are speaking;

(d) Writing – which tests how well you can make yourself understood when you write things down.

As you can see, it is all a matter of understanding and of making yourself understood, just as it would be if you were in France and didn't have an English person to help you.

When you do go to France, you will find yourself surrounded by signs and notices of all kinds, and bombarded by sounds of all kinds. Sometimes, if someone is speaking directly to you, an effort will be made to make it easier for you to understand, and, of course, when you are speaking yourself, French people will usually be patient and help you if you have difficulty expressing yourself.

But newspapers, signs in shops, and radio and television programmes are not designed for foreigners: they are designed for French people, and that means they may be hard for a foreigner to understand.

Life would be pretty dull however if you couldn't get something out of these things, and so you need to try. Fortunately you don't always need to understand every word to get an idea of what it is all about. You will probably find some of the things in this book very difficult to understand at first, but we hope that by the time you have had a bit of practice you will start to find it easier.

Tony Whelpton
Daphne Jenkins

Unit 1
Pour aller à ... ?

In this unit you will learn

– how to ask the way

– how to understand directions you are given

– how to give instructions

When you're in France and you want to ask how to get somewhere, the easiest way to ask is to use the expression

Pour aller à ... ?

Pour aller à la gare, s'il vous plaît?

Pour aller à la rue Saint-Jacques, s'il vous plaît?

1   Practise asking the way to each of these places:

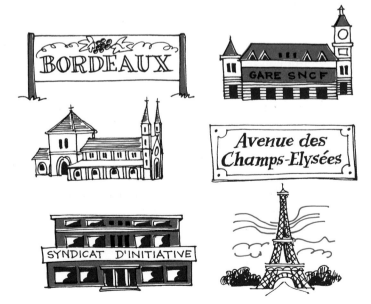

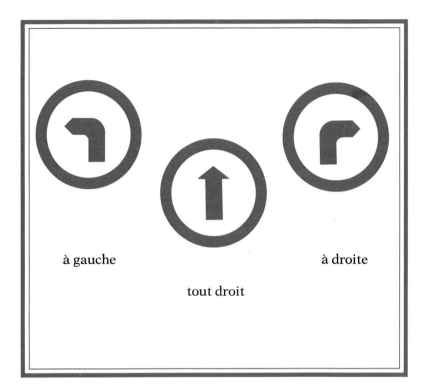

à gauche   à droite

tout droit

2a Listen to the cassette. You will hear a number of people using the expression **Pour aller à ...**, and you will also hear the answers they are given. As you listen, write down the names of the places they want to get to.

2b Look at the information box, then listen to the cassette again and note down the directions the various people were given.

3 Listen to the cassette. You will hear a conversation between a man and a policeman. The man wants to go to the Avenue de l'Opéra, in Paris, and he asks the policeman, 'Pour aller à l'Avenue de l'Opéra, s'il vous plaît?' Listen to the conversation again, then answer these questions:

1. How does the man intend to get there?

2. Which number house does he want to get to?

3. What isn't he sure of?

4. What is the first landmark the policeman tells him to watch out for?

5. How is he to get to this landmark?

3

6. What should he do then?

7. What if he doesn't want to do that?

8. At the Rue Montmartre *métro* station, should he turn right or left?

9. Which roads does he go down then?

 4a Listen to the cassette. You will hear some directions, given to you by someone you are intending to visit. Follow the directions on the little sketch map. Is your friend's flat marked 1, 2, 3 or 4?

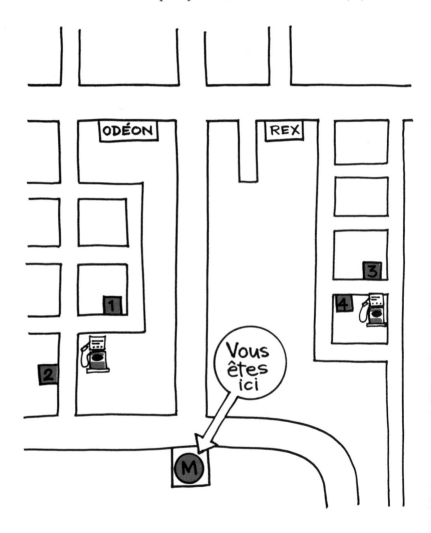

4b Listen to the directions on the cassette again, then look at these statements and say whether they are true or false:

1. Il faut tourner à gauche tout de suite.

2. Vous tournerez à droite au carrefour.

3. Il faut tourner juste avant le cinéma.

4. Tout de suite après le cinéma vous prenez la troisième rue à gauche.

5. Il y a une station-service en face de l'immeuble.

6. L'appartement de votre amie est le numéro trente-huit.

7. Il vous faudra monter au troisième.

8. Il faut sonner deux fois à la porte.

9. Puis vous monterez l'escalier.

5a Listen to the cassette. You will hear some more directions, given this time to a girl in Limoges who is asking someone the way. As you listen, write down the following:

1. where she wants to go;

2. where she is now;

3. which way she should turn after crossing the square;

4. what building she will see as she goes down the Boulevard Carnot;

5. what she has to do when she reaches the Avenue de la Gare.

5b Now listen to the directions again, and write the answers to these questions:

1. Why is the man a little surprised at the girl's question?

2. How does she intend to get to where she is going?

3. Why doesn't she mind how long it takes? (Listen for two reasons.)

4. Where are they standing as they talk?

5. What building is the girl standing in front of?

6. Which way does she have to go after crossing the square?

7. What is the name of the road she has to go down?

8. What two places should she see on her right as she goes down that road?

9. What does she have to do when she gets to the Avenue Garibaldi?

10. Where will she find the Avenue de la Gare?

5

Other ways of asking the way

Où est la gare, s'il vous plaît?

Quel est le chemin de la gare, s'il vous plaît?

Quelle route faut-il prendre pour aller à la gare, s'il vous plaît?

Be polite!

Remember always to add the expression **s'il vous plaît**, and to say **merci** when someone has helped you. And don't forget to call the other person **monsieur**, **madame** or **mademoiselle**.
The other person will usually say something like:

De rien, monsieur.

Je vous en prie, mademoiselle.

Key words for telling someone the way

Instructions

Prenez... (e.g. Prenez l'avenue en face de vous)

Suivez... (e.g. Suivez le Boulevard Montmartre)

Continuez tout droit...

Tournez...

Traversez... (e.g. Traversez l'Avenue Garibaldi)

Directions

en face de vous	*facing you*
devant vous	*in front of you*
derrière vous	*behind you*
tout droit	*straight ahead*
à droite	*on the right*
à gauche	*on the left*
jusqu'à	*as far as*

6a Now look at the map of Auvergne, and say where you would arrive if you followed the instructions.

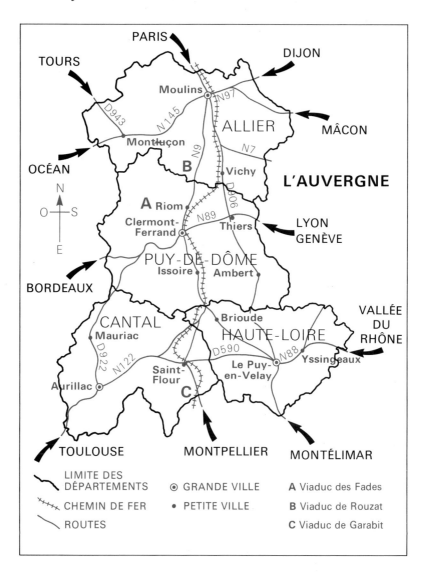

1. Vous êtes à Clermont-Ferrand. Prenez la Route Nationale 9, traversez Riom, et vous vous trouverez à ......

2. Vous êtes à Clermont-Ferrand. Prenez la Route nationale 89 jusqu'à Thiers, puis tournez à gauche. Vous arriverez bientôt à ......

3. Vous êtes à Aurillac. Prenez la Route Départementale 922. Quand vous arriverez à la Route Nationale 89, tournez à droite, traversez Clermont-Ferrand, et juste après le carrefour vous vous trouverez à ......

6b Look at the map of Auvergne again and say how you would tell someone the following:

1. how to get to Yssingeaux from Le Puy-en-Velay;

2. how to get to Clermont-Ferrand from Saint-Flour;

3. how to get to Vichy from Montluçon;

4. how to get to Moulins from Aurillac.

6c Look at the map again, then say whether the following statements are true or false:

1. Clermont-Ferrand se trouve au centre de l'Auvergne.

2. Moulins est dans le département du Puy-de-Dôme.

3. La Route Nationale 89 traverse la Haute-Loire.

4. Le chemin de fer passe par Vichy.

5. Le Viaduc des Fades est au nord du Viaduc de Garabit.

6. Il y a cinq départements en Auvergne.

6d Still looking at the map of Auvergne, answer these questions in French:

1. Quelle est la plus grande ville du Puy-de-Dôme?

2. Quelle route nationale traverse l'Auvergne du nord au sud?

3. Dans quel département se trouve le Viaduc de Rouzat?

4. Combien de départements y a-t-il en Auvergne?

5. Dans quelle ville peut-on prendre quatre routes nationales?

6. Est-ce que le chemin de fer traverse l'Auvergne du nord au sud ou de l'ouest à l'est?

7a Look at the plan of Calais, follow these instructions, and see where they lead you.

Vous êtes au port. Tournez tout de suite à gauche, prenez la première à droite. Après le tournant, ne prenez pas à gauche, mais continuez tout droit jusqu'à l'Hôtel de Ville. Tournez à droite, traversez le carrefour, et sur votre droite vous trouverez la . . . . . .

A   Hoverport

B   Port

C   Hypermarché

D   Hôtel de Ville

E   Gare

F   Place d'Armes

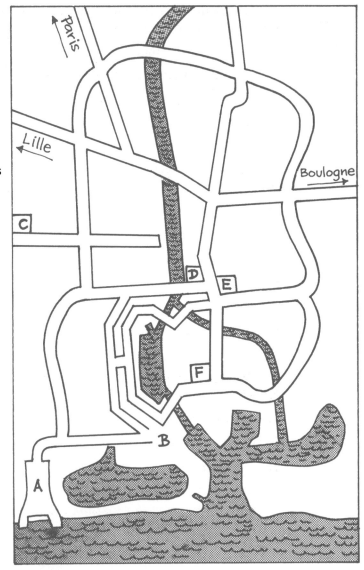

You should have found your way to the Place d'Armes. If you didn't, have another look at the instructions.

 7b Now, still using the plan of Calais, try this with a friend. Choose a starting point, and a place to give directions to. Your friend should look at the map and follow the instructions you give.

1. Tell your friend where he or she is.

2. Give directions.

3. Ask where he or she is now.

7c Now change roles, so that you are looking at the map and your friend is giving the instructions, and try it again.

8 Write down how you would tell someone the following:

1. to cross the Place d'Armes;

2. to turn right at the crossroads;

3. to take the second on the left;

4. to go straight on;

5. to take the first on the right;

6. to turn right just after the cinema;

7. your flat is just opposite the petrol station;

8. to ring twice;

9. you live on the second floor;

10. to come upstairs.

9 Imagine you have been given these directions to find a friend's house, but it is raining and the raindrops have smudged the ink. See if you can write out the instructions fully and correctly.

> Descend_ de l'autobus à ⬤ Place Stanislas.
> Traver_ la Place et pass_ deva_ le cinéma
> ava_ de tourn_ à droite. Pren_ la troisième
> rue à g_che, puis continue tout dro_
> Au ca_efour tu verras une banque. Juste
> après la banque, tourne à droi_ et tu
> verras ma maison juste en f_ d'une pharmacie.
> Ne so_ pas, parce que la sonnette ne marche pas!
> Fra_ très fort et puis je viendrai t'ouvri_ ⬤.

10 Imagine that you are to meet a French friend in Calais. You have arranged to meet at the railway station, and your friend is coming by car from Paris. Write a note to your friend giving directions.

11a While you are on your way somewhere, you are likely to see a lot of signs or notices. Some of them may be helpful, others not, but if they are to be of any use to you at all, you need to understand what they say.

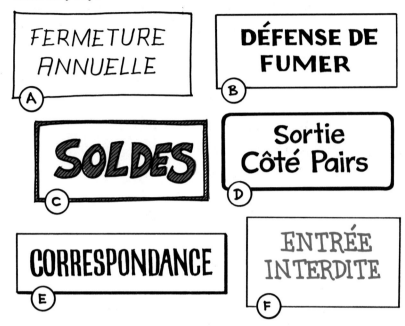

Which of these signs tells you:

1. you mustn't smoke;

2. the owner is on holiday;

3. you mustn't go in by this way;

4. you go out this way if you are looking for the even-numbered buildings of the street;

5. there is a sale on;

6. the way to go if you are changing trains.

11b Which of these explanations goes with which sign?

1. Ça veut dire que si on veut changer de train, on passe par là.

2. Ça veut dire que le propriétaire est en vacances.

3. Ça veut dire qu'ils ont réduit leurs prix.

4. Ça veut dire qu'il faut éteindre sa cigarette.

5. Ça veut dire que si le numéro de la maison qu'on cherche est trente-huit, on sort par là.

6. Ça veut dire qu'il ne faut pas passer par là.

11

Voici le premier épisode d'une histoire intitulée *Les Anges du Diable*. Il y aura un épisode dans chacune des six premières leçons.

— Dis donc, Suzanne! Tout va bien pour ce soir, hein?

— Mais oui, bien sûr! Tu as vu les affiches?

— Non. Fais voir.

— Voilà, je t'en donne une. A tout à l'heure, hein?

Les deux amis, Pierre et Suzanne, sont à l'école, mais aujourd'hui ils ne font pas vraiment attention en classe.

Pourquoi? Eh bien, Pierre joue de la guitare, Suzanne joue de la batterie, et avec deux amis — Catherine, qui chante, et Robert, qui joue aussi de la guitare — ils jouent ensemble aux boums de leurs amis.

Mais aujourd'hui c'est différent: leur groupe, nommé «Les Anges du Diable», donne son premier concert. Ils vont jouer dans une salle du Café Longchamp, et on vend des billets — des gens vont payer pour les entendre jouer!

A l'heure du déjeuner Robert, Catherine et Pierre parlent ensemble dans la cour. Soudain Suzanne arrive en courant.

— Holà, les copains, s'écrie-t-elle. Regardez ceci! Et elle leur indique un bout de papier.
— Qu'est-ce que c'est? demande Pierre.

— Lis cette lettre et tu vas voir! Je n'arrive pas à le croire, moi!

En effet c'est incroyable, parce que cette lettre leur annonce que Michel Henri, disc-jockey bien connu de la station de radio «Europe Numéro Un» vient lui-même à leur concert. Quelle nouvelle!

(A SUIVRE)

Un peu de grammaire

The Imperative

The part of the verb you use to give instructions is called the Imperative.

The Imperative is nearly always the same as the **tu** form or the **vous** form of the present tense, e.g.

suivre: suivez (*as in* suivez cette avenue)

prendre: prends (*as in* prends la première à gauche)

One exception:

Be careful when you write down an instruction to someone you call **tu**. If you are using an **-er** verb, you leave off the **s**, e.g.

tourner: tu tournes: tourne (*as in* tourne à droite)

For once, **aller** behaves like any other **-er** verb, as you can see in the examples below.

So to give an instruction, you say:

aller	va	allez	**suivre**	suis	suivez
descendre	descends	descendez	**tourner**	tourne	tournez
prendre	prends	prenez	**venir**	viens	venez

If you want to tell someone *not* to do something, just put **ne** and **pas** on either side of the verb, e.g.

Ne prends pas la seconde rue à droite.

Ne venez pas avant deux heures.

N'allez pas tout droit.

Reflexive verbs like **se lever, s'asseoir**, etc. add the word **toi** or **vous**, as the case may be, e.g.	If you want to make these negative, though, the form changes as follows:
Lève-toi!	Ne te lève pas!
Assieds-toi!	Ne t'assieds pas!
Couchez-vous!	Ne vous couchez pas!
Arrêtez-vous!	Ne vous arrêtez pas!

Unit 2
Un carnet, s'il vous plaît…

In this unit you will learn how to

– cope with travelling in Paris

– ask someone how to get to a place by public transport

– find out about the different methods of paying fares

– ask about the price of tickets

– buy tickets

– ask questions

1   This map shows how you can travel by train from either of the two main airports into the centre of Paris. Write down:
1. the names of the two airports;
2. at which stations you could change from train to métro.

AÉROGARE 1   AÉROGARE 2

GARE DE ROISSY-
AÉROPORT-CHARLES-DE-GAULLE

Paris ⟷ aérogares

(B)

(A)

LA DÉFENSE
ST-GERMAIN-EN-LAYE

CHARLES DE GAULLE
ÉTOILE   AUBER

(M) GARE DU NORD*

TORCY-
MARNE-LA-VALLÉE
BOISSY-ST-LÉGER

INVALIDES   QUAI
D'ORSAY

CHATELET-LES-HALLES*

NATION

(A)

PT DE L'ALMA

M   CHAMP-DE-MARS

PT ST-MICHEL

GARE DE LYON

JAVEL

LUXEMBOURG

GARE
D'AUSTERLITZ

BD VICTOR

PORT ROYAL

BD MASSÉNA

(C)

VERSAILLES
ST-QUENTIN-
EN-YVELINES

DENFERT-
ROCHEREAU

CITÉ-
UNIVERSITAIRE

(RER)

➤ Ligne (A)

➤ Ligne (B)

➤ Ligne (C)

(B)

ROBINSON
ST-RÉMY-LES-CHEVREUSE

GARE DE PONT-DE-RUNGIS-
AÉROPORT-D'ORLY

AÉROGARE
ORLY OUEST

AÉROGARE ORLY SUD

(M) Gares avec correspondance Métro

* Gare du Nord - Châtelet-les-Halles à partir du 10.12.81
Changement de train quai à quai à Gare du Nord.

15

2a Look at the simplified map of the Paris *métro*. Read the statements in French, then answer the questions.

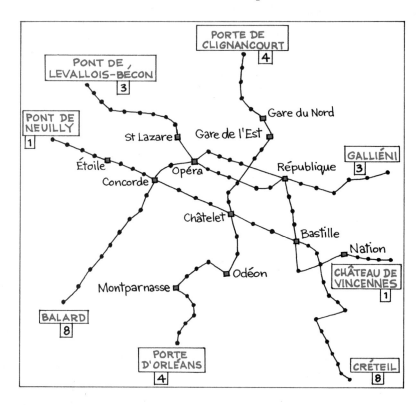

Chaque ligne est désignée par un numéro, ou par le nom de ses terminus. Regardez la ligne numéro huit. Elle va de Balard à Créteil. Alors vous dites « la ligne Balard–Créteil ».

L'indication des directions permet de s'orienter sur les quais et dans les couloirs. Alors, si vous voulez voyager vers Balard, cherchez l'indication « Direction Balard ».

Si vous devez changer de train, cherchez sur le quai l'indication « Correspondance ». Puis cherchez encore l'indication « Direction Balard ».

Les trains mettent à peu près quatre-vingts secondes à voyager d'une station à la prochaine. Alors, comptez en moyenne quatre-vingts secondes de trajet par station.

Le premier train du matin quitte le terminus à cinq heures et demie. La nuit, le dernier train arrive au terminus à une heure et quart.

Le prix des tickets reste toujours le même, même si vous allez loin.

1. How does each line on the *métro* get its name?

2. Where will you find these names displayed?

3. Apart from when you are starting your journey, when might you need to know the name of the line you are travelling on?

4. Roughly how long does it take to travel from one station to the next?

5. At what time does the first train of the day set out?

6. At what time does the last train of the day reach its destination?

7. If you have to pay 4 francs to travel four stations down the line, how much would it cost to travel twelve stations?

2b Here are the names of eight stations, all of which are at the end of a line. Look at the map again, and then write down the name of the station that is at the other end of the line.

1. Balard;

2. Porte de Clignancourt;

3. Château de Vincennes;

4. Pont de Levallois-Bécon;

5. Galliéni;

6. Créteil;

7. Porte d'Orléans;

8. Pont de Neuilly.

 2c Working with a partner, take it in turns to ask each other questions, following this pattern:

—Étoile, c'est sur quelle ligne?

—Numéro 1.

—La ligne numéro 1, c'est quoi?

—Pont de Neuilly–Château de Vincennes.

Asking the way

To find out your route you can simply ask **Pour aller à ... ?**, just as you would in the street, but you would be more likely to say:

Pour aller à Concorde, quelle ligne faut-il prendre, s'il vous plaît?

Or you might say:

Pour aller à Concorde, quelle direction faut-il prendre, s'il vous plaît?

If you want more precise information, such as whether you need to change trains, or where you need to change, you say:

C'est direct?

or Est-ce que j'ai besoin de changer?

or Où faut-il changer?

3 Listen to the cassette. You will hear four short conversations, in which a man asks for advice about how to get somewhere, and a woman gives the required information. In each case, answer these questions:

1. Where does the man want to go?

2. Which line does he need to take?

3. Where, if necessary, does he need to change?

4a Listen to the cassette. You will hear a conversation between a man who has never travelled on the *métro* before, and a friend who is showing him round Paris.

1. Where do they want to get to?

2. Who is going to buy the tickets?

3. How many tickets are there in a *carnet*?

4. Why is it a good idea to buy a *carnet*?

5. How many classes are there on the *métro*?

6. What is the disadvantage of travelling first class?

4b Listen to the cassette again, then say whether these statements are true or false:

1. Les deux amis sont à Concorde.

2. Ils veulent aller à Concorde.

3. Le jeune homme va acheter un seul ticket.

4. C'est plus cher si on achète un carnet.

5. Il y a douze tickets dans un carnet.

6. Il y a deux classes dans le métro.

7. Il est moins cher de voyager en première classe.

Asking the price

The usual question, wherever you are, is

C'est combien?

This may then be followed by whatever you want to know the price of, e.g.

C'est combien, un ticket seconde?

C'est combien, un carnet première?

Buying tickets

Say how many you want, and which class, e.g.

Deux tickets seconde, s'il vous plaît.

Un carnet première, s'il vous plaît.

4c What would you say if you wanted:

1. to know how to get to Jussieu?

2. to know if you need to change to get to Odéon?

3. to know where to change to get to Passy?

4. three first-class tickets?

5. a book of second-class tickets?

5a Work with a partner. One of you is to look at the map of the
métro on page 16, the other is to ask questions which the first
will answer. For example, if you were at Balard, and you wanted
to get to Montparnasse, you would say:

Pour aller à Montparnasse, s'il vous plaît?

The answer would be:

Pour aller à Montparnasse, prenez la direction Créteil, et
changez à Concorde et à Châtelet.

What would the answer be in the following cases:

1. if you were at Odéon and you wanted to get to Étoile?

2. if you were at Étoile and you wanted to get to St Lazare?

3. if you were at St Lazare and you wanted to get to Concorde?

4. if you were at Concorde and you wanted to get to Gare du
   Nord?

5. if you were at Gare du Nord and you wanted to get to Odéon?

5b Still working with a partner, choose a station marked on the
map and decide where you want to get to.

1. Tell your friend where you are.

2. Say where you want to go.

3. Ask for directions.

Now change roles.

6 Practise this situation with a partner. You are at Ternes station.
Your partner will give the answers in brackets.

1. Ask how to get to Gare du Nord.
   (Pont de Neuilly-Château de Vincennes line, going towards
   Neuilly.)

2. Ask if you have to change.
   (Yes, you change onto the Porte d'Orléans–Porte de
   Clignancourt line.)

3. Ask where.
   (Châtelet, and go towards Porte de Clignancourt.)

4. Ask how long it will take to get there.
   (About fifteen minutes.)

7 Write a note to a friend who lives near the Porte de Clignancourt, giving directions for coming to visit you at Créteil.

1. Say which station to start from.

2. Say which line and direction to take.

3. Say where to change.

8 Imagine you are writing to a friend about the Paris *métro*. What would you write if you wanted to tell him or her about the following:

1. the time the trains start running in the morning;

2. the time they finish running at night;

3. how long it takes to travel from Étoile to where you are staying at Passy (it is only four stops);

4. it is cheaper to buy tickets in books of ten.

9a Paris isn't the only city in France to have a *métro*. Look at the information about the *métro* in Lille, in the north of France, then answer the questions.

1. How long does it take to travel between each station?

2. How long would it take to travel from Gares to C.H.R.B. Calmette?

3. How often do the trains run in the rush hour?

4. How often do they run at other times?

9b Look at the information on the Lille *métro* again, then answer the questions in French.

1. Combien de temps faut-il pour voyager d'une station de métro à une autre?

2. Quel voyage dure neuf minutes environ?

3. Quand est-ce qu'il y a le plus grand nombre de trains?

4. Quand est-ce qu'il y a le moins de trains?

10 Listen to the cassette. You will hear a conversation between two friends at a bus stop (= un arrêt d'autobus). When you have listened to the conversation, answer the questions.

1. What bus do they need to get?

2. What does the young man think you need to do when you get on the bus?

3. Why doesn't he need to do this?

4. How many tickets do they need for this journey?

5. What must they do with the tickets when they get on the bus?

6. By which door will they have to enter the bus?

7. What would they have to do if they did not have tickets already?

11 Read this information about the Parisian bus system, then say whether the statements which follow are true or false.

Chaque ligne d'autobus est divisée en sections qui déterminent le prix du trajet: un ticket jusqu'à deux sections, deux tickets au-delà, jusqu'à quatre tickets sur les lignes de banlieue. Le carnet de dix tickets (valable aussi dans le métro) s'achète dans les stations de métro, dans les bureaux de tabac, dans certaines boutiques ou dans les autobus comportant un receveur.

1. To travel by bus, you may need more than one ticket per person.

2. You need to buy a ticket for every fare stage travelled.

3. You will never need more than four tickets for one journey.

4. Bus tickets may be used in the *métro* as well.

5. You can only buy bus tickets in *métro* stations.

6. You can buy bus tickets at a tobacconist's shop.

7. You have to buy your tickets from the bus conductor.

12 Listen to the cassette. You will hear a conversation between a Parisian taxi-driver and a man who has just got into his cab. When you have heard it, answer the questions.

1. What does the taxi-driver want to know first?

2. Where does the man want to go to eventually?

3. Where does he need to stop off first?

4. What train does he want to catch?

5. What is causing hold-ups in some streets today?

6. How long would the journey normally take?

7. How long is it likely to take today?

8. At what time is the man due to pick up his colleague?

13a Listen to the cassette. You will hear an announcement to drivers broadcast on the radio. When you have heard it, answer the questions.

1. To whom exactly is the announcement addressed?

2. What has caused a hold-up in the Avenue Mozart?

3. Where is the Avenue Mozart?

4. What exactly happened?

5. What are motorists advised to do?

6. When do they hope it will be clear?

13b Work with a partner. An English person is staying with a friend in Paris. The friend is shortly going out by car, and would normally drive along the Avenue Mozart. The English visitor has heard the announcement, but the friend has not. Decide which of you will play which part, then the English person will tell the friend what he/she has heard, and answer his/her questions. Prepare what you are going to say beforehand.

NOTRE FEUILLETON

Voici le second épisode des *Anges du Diable*.

Résumé: Quatre jeunes musiciens, Catherine, Suzanne, Robert et Pierre, ont formé un groupe nommé «Les Anges du Diable». Ce soir ils vont donner leur premier concert, et ils ont été étonnés de recevoir une lettre annonçant que Michel Henri, disc-jockey célèbre, va assister lui-même à leur concert.

Les quatre Anges du Diable discutent vivement ensemble la nouvelle qu'ils viennent de recevoir. Soudain ils entendent une autre voix: c'est un autre élève, Albert Duval. C'est Catherine qui le remarque la première, et elle chuchote:

—Dis donc! Voilà Albert Duval! Il nous écoute!
—Qu'est-ce que vous avez là? Pourquoi vous criez tous comme des imbéciles? demande Albert.
—Va t'en, Albert! Ça ne te regarde pas! crie Catherine.

La réponse de Catherine n'est peut-être pas très polie, mais Albert Duval n'est plus un ami des Anges. Au commencement il jouait avec le groupe, mais il ne jouait pas très bien et Pierre lui a dit qu'ils ne voulaient plus de lui.

Depuis, il fait tout son possible pour être désagréable.
—Vous allez regretter ça! s'écrie Albert.
—Hé, pourquoi? demande Suzanne.
—Vous allez voir! dit Albert. Puis il s'en va.

—Qu'est-ce qu'il veut dire? demande
Suzanne.
—Rien, Suzy, ne t'en fais pas. Il ne
peut rien faire, répond Pierre.

—Allez, il est presque deux heures, il
faut rentrer. A quatre heures, hein?
dit Pierre.
—D'accord, répondent les autres.

A quatre heures, trois des Anges se
retrouvent dans la cour de l'école.
Mais Pierre n'est pas là.
—Où donc est Pierre? dit Robert.

—Le voici qui arrive, répond
Catherine. Mais qu'est-ce qu'il a? Il a
l'air vraiment mécontent.

Pierre arrive, salue les amis.
—Mais qu'est-ce que tu as, Pierre? Il
y a quelque chose qui ne va pas? lui

demande Catherine.
—C'est ma guitare... je l'ai perdue!

(A SUIVRE)

Un peu de grammaire

Asking questions

To check that you've got something right, just add **n'est-ce pas?** or **c'est ça?**

Nous allons prendre le numéro 73, n'est-ce pas?

Nous allons à Concorde, c'est ça?

To change a statement into a question, just raise your voice at the end of the sentence.

J'achète un ticket au receveur?

You can also add the words **Est-ce que** at the beginning of the sentence:

Est-ce que j'achète un ticket au receveur?

Or else you can turn the verb round, e.g.

Voulez-vous descendre à Opéra?

If you want to ask when, where, why, what or how, you simply use the following words with one of the forms shown above, e.g.

Quand (= *when*) est-ce que je descends?

Où (= *where*) est-ce que je vous emmène?

Pourquoi (= *why*) voulez-vous aller à Châtelet?

Que (= *what*) veux-tu faire aujourd'hui?
(*or* Qu'est-ce que tu veux faire aujourd'hui?)

Comment (= *how*) est-ce que je vais trouver ta maison?

Unit 3
Chez soi

In this unit you will learn how to

- tell others about your home

- find out similar details from others

- tell others about the area where you live

- ask them about the area where they live

- talk about your everyday routine at home

 1a Look at the picture and plan of a house, then say whether the statements are true or false.

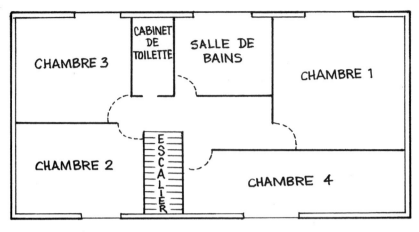

PREMIER ÉTAGE

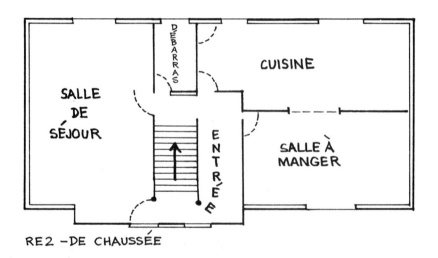

REZ-DE CHAUSSÉE

1. C'est une maison à trois étages.

2. Au premier étage il y a quatre fenêtres.

3. Il n'y a pas de cheminée.

4. La salle de bains est au rez-de-chaussée.

5. Le cabinet de toilette est au premier étage.

6. Le cabinet de toilette est en face de l'escalier.

7. La maison compte quatre chambres à coucher.

8. La salle à manger est plus grande que la salle de séjour.

9. La salle de séjour est à droite de la porte d'entrée.

10. La cuisine est moins grande que la salle à manger.

1b Look at the plan of the house again, and answer the questions in French.

1. Combien de pièces y a-t-il au premier étage?

2. Quelles sont ces pièces?

3. Combien de pièces y a-t-il au rez-de-chaussée?

4. Quelles sont ces pièces?

5. Dans quelle pièce est-ce qu'on mange?

6. Dans quelle pièce est-ce qu'on se lave?

7. Où se trouve la cuisine?

8. Où se trouve la salle de bains?

9. Quelle petite pièce se trouve entre la cuisine et la salle de séjour?

10. Comment est-ce qu'on arrive au premier étage?

2a Now think about your own house or flat, or, if you prefer, the house of someone you know, and say whether these statements are true or false:

1. C'est une maison à deux étages.

2. La salle de bains est au rez-de-chaussée.

3. Le cabinet de toilette est au premier étage.

4. Le cabinet de toilette est en face de l'escalier.

5. La maison compte deux chambres à coucher.

6. La salle de séjour est moins grande que la salle à manger.

7. La maison n'a pas de jardin.

8. La cuisine est plus grande que la salle à manger.

2b Still thinking about the same house, write answers in French to these questions:

1. Combien de pièces y a-t-il?

2. Quelles sont ces pièces?

3. Dans quelle pièce est-ce que vous mangez?

4. Dans quelle pièce est-ce que vous vous lavez?

5. Où se trouve la cuisine?

6. Où se trouve la salle de bains?

29

2c Working with a friend, take it in turns to ask each other questions about where you live.

3 Listen to the cassette recording in which you will hear a French boy talking about where he lives, then answer the questions.

1. Why doesn't the girl know whether Pierre's house is big or not?

2. Does Pierre live in a house or a flat?

3. On which floor does he live?

4. Where is Choisy-le-Roi?

5. Why doesn't Pierre use the stairs?

6. How many bedrooms are there?

7. What other rooms are there?

8. Which one is Pierre's?

9. Which one do his parents sleep in?

10. Who has the other one?

11. When?

12. Why don't they have their own garden?

4a Imagine a French person has said to you, 'Parlez-moi un peu de votre maison'. What would you say?

4b Write three short sentences about your house or flat, using as a guide the questions you have just been asking and answering.

4c Imagine that you have just received this letter from a new French pen-friend. Write a letter in reply, answering the questions she asks.

Cher ------

Saint-Cézaire-sur-Siagne, le 28 mars

Merci de ta lettre que j'ai reçue hier. Je suis très contente d'avoir un correspondant anglais et j'espère que nous nous verrons un jour. Malheureusement je suis sur le point de partir en Italie pendant quelques jours et je n'ai pas le temps de t'écrire plus longuement, mais je promets de t'écrire aussitôt que je reviendrai. Je t'envoie ma photo, et aussi une photo de ma maison. Comme tu vois, elle est grande, et il y a une piscine. J'espère qu'un jour tu viendras passer les vacances ici - ça te plairait? Toi, tu habites une maison ou un appartement? Dans ta prochaine lettre, fais-moi une petite description de là où tu habites - je m'intéresse beaucoup aux demeures des gens. Eh bien, maman m'appelle pour partir. Alors je te dis au revoir.

Ton amie française
Nicolette

5   Look at the advertisement for houses for sale in the South of France, then say whether the statements are true or false.

Maisons de pêcheurs.

325.000 F

Votre maison 3 pièces + jardin privatif à proximité d'un authentique village méridional. Existe aussi en 4 et 5 pièces. Prix fermes et définitifs à la réservation. Crédit 15 ans par l'UCB-CFEC.   *à partir de

JACQUES RIBOUREL
Méditerranée
J.R.S.A. – 120, Champs-Élysées, 75008 Paris. 562.00.90.

Veuillez m'envoyer votre documentation "Sausset-les-Pins".

Nom : _____ Adresse : _____

Tél. : _____ Tél. bureau : _____

1. Some of these houses have three rooms, others have more.

2. The owners have to share a garden.

3. At the moment the houses are occupied by fishermen.

4. They have been built on the outskirts of a large town.

5. You can spread the payments over fifteen years.

6 Look at another advertisement for properties for sale, then answer the questions.

1. What sort of people is the advertisement aimed at?

2. What does the advertisement say you should do about your present home?

3. Why?

4. In what sort of place are these houses situated?

5. How far is it from Paris?

6. How many rooms do the houses have?

7. On what days could you not go to see them?

8. On what day could you go to look at them in the morning?

7a Look at this plan of part of a town. Which of the places marked do each of the sentences refer to?

1. C'est ici qu'on va si on est très malade.

2. C'est ici qu'on va si on veut poster des lettres.

3. C'est ici qu'on va si on veut étudier.

4. C'est ici qu'on va si on veut voir un film.

5. C'est ici qu'on va si on veut jouer au football ou au tennis.

6. C'est ici qu'on va si on va se marier.

7. C'est ici qu'on va si on veut voir un opéra.

8. C'est ici qu'on va si on veut emprunter des livres.

9. C'est ici qu'on va si on veut se baigner.

10. C'est ici qu'on va si on veut passer la soirée avec ses copains.

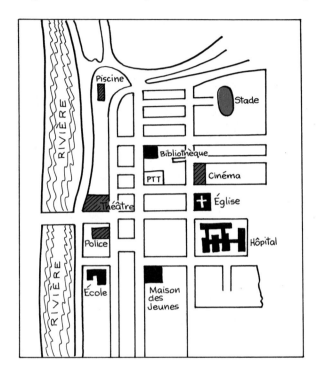

 7b Now write down the answers to these questions:

1. Que fait-on à l'église?

2. Que fait-on au cinéma?

3. Que fait-on à l'école?

4. Que fait-on au stade?

5. Que fait-on à la piscine?

6. Quand est-ce qu'on va à l'hôpital?

7. Pourquoi va-t-on à la Maison des Jeunes?

8. Pourquoi va-t-on à la bibliothèque?

7c Write down four or five sentences in French saying what sort of buildings there are near where you live, and what you would do there.

33

8 Try this with a friend. Think of a place you might find in a town.
   Your friend has to ask you questions in French about what you
   would do there, when you would go there, etc., and try and work
   out what building you are thinking of. Then change places. Here
   is an example:

   —Je pense à un endroit près de chez moi.

   —Tu y vas pour voir des films?

   —Non.

   —Quel jour de la semaine y vas-tu?

   —Dimanche et mercredi.

   —Tu y vas pour prier?

   —Non.

   —Pourquoi y vas-tu?

   —Pour jouer au football.

   —C'est le stade?

   —Oui, c'est le stade.

If you look at a French telephone number, you will see that
it is split up into little bits, e.g. 49.13.11. This is to make it
easier to say. Instead of saying each figure separately, as
we do in England, the French would treat each of these
bits separately, and say **Quarante-neuf, treize, onze**.
There is one way in which it is different from using
ordinary numbers: you might find a number beginning
with 0, e.g. 03. In this case you would say **Zéro trois**.

9a Look at the notice from a local newspaper about various
    services which are available in and around Cannes. Practise
    saying in French all the telephone numbers that are given.

9b Work with a partner. Each of you should write a list of telephone
    numbers. Take it in turns to give a number, which the other
    must write down, and then check if they are correct.

Bloc-notes de Cannes et sa périphérie

JOURNÉE DU SAMEDI 14 AOUT 1983

MÉDECINS

—**S.O.S. Médecins** (24 heures sur 24). – Tél. 38.39.38.

—**Hôtel de police,** 15, avenue de Grasse, à Cannes, tél. 39.10.78.

Mandelieu. – Jusqu'au lundi 8 h : Dr Guillere, tél. 49.03.11 ou 49.53.96.

Mougins. – Jusqu'à lundi 8 h : Dr Galy, tél. 90.01.77.

PHARMACIES

De permanence mais à guichets fermés pour Cannes et les communes environnantes:

Dimanche, de 9 h à 19 h 30 : Altouvas, 46, rue d'Antibes.

Lundi, de 9 h à 19 h 30 : Pappochia, 23, avenue de Lérins.

A partir de 19 h 30 et exclusivement pour les ordonnances urgentes, se présenter au commissariat central, 15, avenue de Grasse, à Cannes.

CHIRURGIENS-DENTISTES

—**Ce dimanche** : Dr Cochais, tél. 39.62.83.

—**Ce lundi** : Dr Medioni, tél. 43.27.66.

—**Pour Mandelieu** : Dr Kayati, tél. 49.82.90.

SERVICES D'URGENCE

Hôtel de police. – 15, avenue de Grasse, à Cannes, tél. 39.10.78.

Pompiers. – Tél. 18 ou 47.61.11.

Police secours. – Tél. 17.

Hôpital. – Tél. 69.91.33.

Gendarmerie. – Tél. 68.01.01.

Affaires maritimes. – Tél. 39.28.39.

Secours en mer. – Poste principal quai Laubeuf, tél. 68.91.92, poste 204; ouvert de 9 h 30 à 19 h 30.

S.O.S. Vétérinaires. – Tél. 83.46.64 (jour et nuit), vous indiquera le ou les vétérinaires de garde.

NUMÉROS D'APPEL

SERVICES DU TOURISME-O.T.S.I.-ACCUEIL DE FRANCE. – 1) Gare S.N.C.F. (tél. 99.19.77), ouvert tous les jours de 8 h à 21 h.
—2) Palais Croisette, 50, boulevard de la Croisette, tél. 39.24.53: ouvert tous les jours de 9 h à 20 h.
—3) Palais des festivals, 1, La Croisette, tél. 39.01.01, poste 3.637: ouvert tous les jours de 9 h à 19 h.
—4) Autoroute, sortie Mougins-Cannes, tél. 45.58.56, ouvert du lundi au samedi, de 10 h à 20 h; dimanches et jours fériés, de 10 h à 13 h et de 15 h à 20 h.

9c Look again at the details of local services in and around Cannes. If you lived there, what telephone number would you ring in each of these cases:

1. if you needed a doctor urgently;

2. if you had tooth-ache;

3. if you needed some medicine urgently;

4. if you needed the fire brigade;

5. if you wanted to find out about train times;

6. if you wanted tourist information;

7. if your dog was badly hurt;

8. if you saw someone in trouble in the sea;

9. if your flat had been broken into;

10. if your friend had had a bad accident.

10a Work with a partner. Each of you is to write down in French:

    1. some details of the house or flat he/she lives in;

    2. what other places are nearby;

    3. what there is to do in the town;

    4. what he/she would like to do at the weekend.

10b Then imagine you are going to stay with the other person, never having visited the town before. Act out a phone call, in which you ask:

    1. what sort of house or flat he/she lives in;

    2. what other places are nearby;

    3. what there is to do in the town;

    4. how he/she would like to spend the weekend.

10c Now change roles, with your partner asking the questions and you giving the answers.

10d Using the details you were given on the phone, write a description of your friend's house or flat and of the town; then compare your version with your partner's original notes.

11 Listen to the cassette recording in which you will hear a conversation between a man and his wife, then answer the questions.

    1. What does the woman ask her husband to do?

    2. What colour roses do they have in their garden?

    3. Which ones have nearly all gone?

    4. Which ones have just come into flower?

    5. What does the husband ask his wife to get?

    6. Where will she have to get it from?

    7. Who put it there?

    8. When?

    9. Why doesn't he want to water the flower-beds yet?

   10. Why does she apologise?

12 Listen to the cassette recording in which you will hear a conversation between a boy and his mother, then answer the questions.

1. Why does Pierre object to laying the table to begin with?

2. What does he ask his mother?

3. What time are they due to eat?

4. What is special about this evening?

5. How many will be eating?

6. How many glasses does he need to put out?

7. What are they going to have for their first course?

8. Where does she want him to get the parsley and thyme from?

9. What is Pierre not sure of?

10. What does his mother do to help him?

13a Listen to the cassette recording in which you will hear a telephone conversation between two girls, then answer the questions.

1. What relation are the girls to each other?

2. Why is Josiane ringing?

3. Is she sad or happy?

4. When is she coming?

5. When is she going back?

6. What time does her train leave Paris?

7. What time does it arrive?

8. What does Sylvie promise to do?

9. What does Josiane want to know?

10. Why doesn't she have time to hear the answer?

13b Work out with a friend how you would perhaps have answered Josiane's questions.

13c Imagine you are Sylvie, and write a letter to Josiane telling her what you didn't have time to tell her on the phone.

NOTRE FEUILLETON

Voici le troisième épisode des *Anges du Diable*.

Les quatre amis, inquiets, commencent à chercher la guitare perdue: s'ils ne la trouvent pas ils devront abandonner le concert; s'ils abandonnent le concert, Michel Henri, le célèbre disc-jockey, viendra pour rien et les Anges du Diable perdront cette belle occasion de lui montrer leur talent. Ils cherchent partout, mais ils ne trouvent pas la guitare.

Enfin, trois quarts d'heure plus tard, quand ils sont sur le point d'accepter qu'ils ne vont pas la trouver, Catherine entre dans les toilettes des filles—et c'est là qu'elle trouve la guitare de Pierre!

Les Anges sortent enfin de l'école. Ils vont tout de suite dans la direction du Café Longchamp. Ils veulent regarder la salle où ils vont jouer, vérifier que tout va bien et répéter quelques-unes de leurs chansons.

Ils arrivent bientôt au café, disent bonjour au patron et entrent dans la salle où ils vont donner le concert.

Suzanne installe la batterie, Pierre et Robert branchent leurs guitares et Catherine prend le micro.

—Attends! crie Pierre soudain. On n'a pas allumé les spots!
Robert va donc les allumer.

Lorsque Robert revient, il reprend sa guitare et les Anges commencent à jouer et à chanter.

Soudain tout est noir et la musique cesse; seuls les tambours continuent un petit moment.
—Qu'est-ce que c'est? crie Catherine.
—C'est l'électricité! répond Pierre. On l'a coupée!

(A SUIVRE)

Un peu de grammaire

Y and **en** are pronouns, and usually go in front of verbs. Like all pronouns, they are standing in for something else.

Y usually takes the place of a whole phrase, e.g.

Je vais au stade pour jouer au football.

Je vais dans la salle de bains pour me laver.

The expressions **au stade** and **dans la salle de bains** say *where* something takes place. But if someone asks you:

Pourquoi vas-tu au stade?

it is a bit boring to repeat **au stade** in your answer, so you replace it by the pronoun **y**, and say:

J'**y** vais pour jouer au football.

En is similar, except that the expression it replaces usually begins with **de**, e.g.

J'**en** ai mis au frigo
stands for
J'ai mis de la bière au frigo;

Veux-tu m'**en** chercher au jardin, s'il te plaît?
stands for
Veux-tu me chercher du persil au jardin, s'il te plaît?

En can also replace the noun when a number is used, e.g.

Il **en** a mangé deux.

– The pronoun **en** stands here for whatever it is he ate two of, i.e. you might say this instead of saying

Il a mangé deux pommes.

Y and **en** can be used together, and they always come in that order, **y** first, then **en**, e.g.

J'**y en** ai mis.

Veux-tu m'**y en** chercher, s'il te plaît?

i.e. you might say this instead of saying

J'ai mis de la viande au four.

or Veux-tu me chercher des fleurs dans le jardin, s'il te plaît?

Unit 4
A l'école

In this unit you will learn how to

- greet other people

- introduce people to each other

- tell others about your daily routine

- ask others about their daily routine

- tell others about your likes and dislikes

- ask others about their likes and dislikes

1 Read this passage, then answer the questions that follow.

C'est le quinze septembre. C'est donc la rentrée des classes après les grandes vacances. Jean et Hélène rentrent au C.E.S. Michelet dans la banlieue de Paris. En route pour l'école ils rencontrent des amis qu'ils n'ont pas vus depuis le mois de juillet. Voici leur conversation:

—Salut, Jean! Salut, Hélène! Ça va?
—Salut, Chantal! Salut, Michel! Oui, ça va très bien! Et vous?
—Formidable! Mais je ne suis pas content de rentrer.
—Moi non plus.

1. What is the date?

2. What happens on that date?

3. What is the C.E.S. Michelet?

4. Where is it?

5. What are Jean and Hélène doing when they meet their friends?

6. When did they last see them?

7. What feelings do they express?

2　Listen to the cassette. You will hear some more pupils going back to school after the summer holidays. Listen to their conversation, then answer the questions.

1. What is Robert's surname?

2. How do you know?

3. Where does Peter come from?

4. How has M. Grimaud heard about Peter?

5. Who does M. Grimaud introduce to the boys?

3a　Here is a conversation in which a boy meets the father of one of his friends, but what the father says has been missed out. Look at it carefully, then working with a friend, try and work out what the man said to the boy. Write down what you decide.

—......
—Bonjour, monsieur.
—......
—Je vais très bien, merci. Et vous?
—......
—Oui, merci, monsieur.
—......
—Sur la Côte d'Azur.
—......
—Oui, il a fait très beau, monsieur.
—......
—Hier, monsieur. Nous avons passé la nuit de mardi dans le train.

3b　Listen to the cassette. You will hear that conversation in full. As you listen, check what you have written, then answer these questions:

1. What is the boy's name?

2. Where had he been on holiday?

3. What was the weather like?

4. When did he come back?

5. How did he travel?

6. What did he do on Tuesday night?

42

Greetings!

To say 'Hello!' or 'Hi!' to close friends, simply say:

Salut!

To say 'Hello!' to someone you don't know very well, or someone much older than you, say:

Bonjour!

To be polite, you should really say:

Bonjour, monsieur!

Bonjour, madame!

Bonjour, mademoiselle!

To ask how a friend is, say:

Ça va?

Comment ça va?

Comment vas-tu?

With someone older, or someone you don't know very well, say:

Comment allez-vous?

If someone says one of these to you, say:

Ça va, merci.

Très bien, merci.

To be polite, say:

Très bien, merci, monsieur.

Très bien, merci, madame.

Très bien, merci, mademoiselle.

Then ask how the other person is too:

Et toi?

Et vous?

4a Here is part of a conversation in which a boy is talking to a friend and is introduced to some other people. Imagine you are the boy, and decide what you would have said. Write down what you decide.

—Papa, je te présente mon nouveau camarade, François Chauvin.
—Enchanté, François. Comment vas-tu?
—......
—Très bien, merci. Tu connais ma fille?
—......
—Alors je te présente Marianne, la sœur de Jules.   *Wld you like*
—......   *to join in (make a party) or a game of*
—Salut! Tu viens faire une partie de tennis ce soir?
—......
—Oh, c'est dommage. Il habite loin, ton grand-père?
—......
—Aujourd'hui?
—......
—Quatre-vingt-dix ans! Oh, la, la, c'est incroyable!

4b Listen to the cassette. You will hear that conversation in full. Check what you have written, then answer the questions.

1. What is the boy's name?

2. Who does the man introduce to him?

3. Who is she?

4. What does she ask him to do?

5. When?

6. Why can't he accept the invitation?

7. Where does his grandfather live?

8. Why is he going to see him?

9. How old is his grandfather?

10. What does Marianne's father think about it?

Introducing people

If you want to introduce someone to someone else you say either:

Je vous présente ...

Je te présente...

or Voici...

– followed by the person's name. (Which of those you use depends on how well you know the other person.)

If you're not sure whether the two people know each other already, you say:

Est-ce que vous connaissez...?

or Tu connais...?

Then, if you find out they don't know each other, you introduce them as above.

If you are introduced to someone, the polite thing to say as you shake hands (which you must always do in France), is:

Enchanté(e), monsieur/madame/mademoiselle.

But it is all right too just to say:

Bonjour, monsieur/madame/mademoiselle.

If you want to be extra polite or formal, you say:

Je suis enchanté(e) de faire votre connaissance.

But if it is a young person of your own age, you would be more likely just to say:

Salut,...!

5 Practise all these expressions, working in groups of three or four people, and taking it in turns to introduce and to be introduced.

6a Look at the school time-table, then answer the questions.

Nom: Duparc Françoise					
	Lundi	Mardi	Mercredi	Jeudi	Vendredi	Samedi
0815	Français	Dessin	—	Math.	⎱ Travaux	Sciences naturelles
0915	Math.	Anglais	—	Géographie	⎰ manuels	Français
Récréation						
1030	Histoire	Sciences naturelles	—	Français	Musique	Math.
1130	Education physique	Français	—	Espagnol	Math.	Anglais
Déjeuner						
1400	Instruction civique	Math.	—	Anglais	Histoire	—
1500	Espagnol	Géographie	—	Travaux dirigés	Anglais	—
1600	Dessin	Espagnol	—	Education physique	—	—

1. What is the name of the pupil whose time-table is shown?

2. What day does she have no lessons?

3. What day does she have the afternoon off?

4. How many periods of French does she have each week?

5. How many periods does she spend on other languages?

6. What other languages does she do?

7. What does she have first thing on a Friday morning?

8. What does she have last period on a Monday afternoon?

6b Look at the time-table again, and then rewrite these sentences, filling in the gaps where necessary.

1. Lundi matin, à huit heures et quart, Françoise étudie le ......

2. Chaque jour, entre dix heures et quart et dix heures et demie, Françoise ......

3. Jeudi matin, après le cours de français, Françoise ......

4. Françoise a un cours de dessin ...... fois par semaine.

5. Mercredi, Françoise ne ...... pas à l'école.

6. Samedi après-midi, Françoise n'a pas de ......

7. Chaque jour, entre midi et demi et deux heures, Françoise ......

8. Vendredi matin, Françoise passe ...... heures à faire les travaux manuels.

46

6c Write out your own school time-table in the same way as the one in the book, using the French names for each subject. If you do some subjects which have not been mentioned here, your teacher will tell you what they are called in French.

7a Listen to the cassette recording in which you will hear a girl being interviewed about what she does at school, then say whether these statements are true or false:

1. She never has any lessons before nine o'clock. F *cours*

à l'heure = on time

2. She usually starts at eight o'clock. T

3. She is sometimes late for school. T

4. Even if pupils are late they are not punished. F *punir*

5. Late pupils are given extra work to do. T

6. She doesn't mind whether she is late or not. F

7. She isn't very keen on work. T

7b Listen to that interview again, and then write down in French the answers to these questions:

1. De quoi la dame veut-elle lui parler?

2. A quelle heure commence-t-elle généralement le travail?

3. Les autres jours, à quelle heure a-t-elle son premier cours?

4. Qu'est-ce qu'on lui fait quand elle est en retard? *late*

5. Alors qu'est-ce qu'elle fait pour éviter ça? *avoid*

6. Que pense-t-elle du travail?

8a Listen to the cassette. You will hear the continuation of the same interview. Listen carefully to the girl's likes and dislikes, and how she says whether she likes a subject or not, then answer the questions.

1. What is her favourite subject? *le dessin - art*

2. Why does she like it?

3. What subject can't she stand?

4. What does she think of maths?

5. Which languages does she study?

6. Which one does she prefer?

8b Now write in French the answers to these questions, e.g.
   Q. Que pense-t-elle du dessin?
   A. Elle l'adore.

1. Que pense-t-elle du dessin?

2. Que pense-t-elle des math?

3. Que pense-t-elle de la biologie?

4. Que pense-t-elle de l'anglais?

5. Que pense-t-elle de l'espagnol?

8c Practise with a friend asking and answering the question **Que penses-tu de...?** (asking about a different school subject each time). Make sure that in your answer you use a verb and that you don't repeat the name of the subject you're talking about.

8d With a friend, practise a conversation along these lines:

1. Ask what time school normally starts.

2. Ask what lesson he/she has on ... day at ... o'clock.

3. Ask what is his/her favourite subject.
   matière

4. Ask what he/she thinks of ...

9 Look at the magazine advertisement for books for sale, then answer the questions.

48

1. What two claims are made by this publisher?

2. What is the English title of the book by George Orwell?

3. How many books are published by Folio for the first time?

4. What is Marcel Aymé's book about?

10a Look at the magazine advertisement for a new calculator, then write down the expressions which mean:

Plus géniale qu'une calculatrice, voici la Math-Machine:

TEXAS INSTRUMENTS TI-30 GALAXY

Dans les tiroirs, les calculatrices : voici la Math-Machine, la nouvelle TI-30 Galaxy de Texas Instruments.

Comparée aux autres, elle est vraiment géniale : nouveau "look", nouveau design, nouvelle approche dans les calculs ; pour des maths plus simples et des résultats plus brillants.

Son clavier est spécialement conçu pour vous éviter

les fautes de frappes, et son affichage, c'est du jamais vu.

Avec la Math-Machine, à vous deux les maths : tout ce qu'elle vous apporte de nouveau est détaillé

Spécifications :
* 66 fonctions dont les statistiques ;
* Affichage incliné - 11 chiffres de précision ;
* Mémoire permanente* ;
* 15 niveaux de parenthèses ;
* 2 ans de garantie ;
* Étui protecteur rigide ;
* Affichage des opérations en attente (Système AOS)*

* Marque déposée Texas Instruments

dans un manuel d'utilisation très complet.

Pour toutes ces raisons, essayez la nouvelle TI-30 Galaxy : vous n'aurez pas de mal à comprendre pourquoi on l'appelle la Math-Machine.

TEXAS INSTRUMENTS

1. more ingenious than a calculator;

2. put your calculators away in a drawer;

3. its keyboard is specially designed;

4. hitting the wrong key;

5. you won't have difficulty understanding;

10b Look at the calculator advertisement again, then answer these questions:

1. Apart from its 'look', what two other things do the makers claim to be new about this calculator?

2. For how long is it guaranteed?

3. If you buy one, what will you be given to help you use it?

4. What do they say you won't find difficult to understand?

5. According to the advertisement, what should you now do with other calculators?

6. What kind of results do they claim for their calculator?

7. What is the keyboard designed to avoid?

8. What is the protective cover like?

11 Listen to the cassette. You will hear two girls talking as they come back to school after the summer holidays. Choose the correct answers to the questions from the options given.

1. What does Chantal want to know first?
   A where Helen went on holiday.
   B what she did when she was on holiday.
   C when she is going on holiday.
   D whether she had a good holiday.

2. What sort of holiday does Helen think Chantal had?
   A fantastic.
   B quite good.
   C dreadful.
   D she didn't have a holiday.

3. What mistake was she making?
   A the word **terrible** means 'fantastic', not 'terrible'.
   B Chantal did go on holiday after all.
   C she thought Chantal was going to England for her holidays.
   D she thought Chantal had had a good holiday.

4. How long did Helen spend in England during the holidays?
   A the whole of the holiday.
   B a week.
   C a fortnight.
   D a month.

5. Where did she go then?
   A Paris.
   B the South of France.
   C abroad.
   D nowhere special.

6. What does Chantal's father do for a living?
   A travel agent.
   B swimming-pool attendant.
   C restaurant owner.
   D waiter.

7. Why couldn't he go on holiday?
   A too much work.
   B didn't want to.
   C couldn't afford it.
   D had to go to England.

8. What did Chantal do to help her father?
   A went shopping.
   B typed letters.
   C cleaned his car.
   D worked in the restaurant.

9. How could Helen see that Chantal had been going to the swimming pool?
   A her hair was wet.
   B she was sunburnt.
   C she was wearing a swimsuit.
   D Chantal's father had told her.

10. What did Helen do on 15 August?
    A went to the seaside.
    B came back to Paris.
    C went to the swimming pool.
    D came back from England.

12 Read this newspaper item about a French schoolgirl, then answer the questions.

Au début de janvier 1982 une jeune fille souriante a repris sa place sur les bancs d'un collège à Nice, pour commencer le nouveau trimestre scolaire. Sabrina Belleval, jolie blonde de seize ans, avait bien des raisons pour sourire parce qu'elle venait de gagner un concours de beauté assez important, celui de toute la France. En effet, on avait élu cette belle collégienne «Miss France».

1. When did this take place?

2. What was Sabrina Belleval like?

3. How did she show that she was pleased?

4. What was she about to begin?

5. What had she just won?

6. Why was this quite important?

Voici le quatrième épisode des *Anges du Diable*.

Sans lumière les Anges ne peuvent pas continuer; d'ailleurs il faut de l'électricité aussi pour les guitares. Ils vont donc chercher le patron du café.

—Ne vous inquiétez pas, dit-il. Ce n'est rien. J'ai appelé un électricien et il s'occupe déjà de la réparation.

Deux minutes plus tard les lumières se rallument et les amis reprennent leurs guitares. Après avoir répété quelques chansons, ils vont dans le café pour prendre quelque chose à boire.

—Tu as peur, Cathy? demande Pierre.
—Mais non, répond-elle. Et toi?
—Mais non, pas du tout, dit Pierre. Mais à vrai dire ils ont tous un peu peur: ils ont le «trac», dit-on,—c'est normal avant de donner un concert, n'est-ce pas?—mais personne n'ose l'admettre.

Enfin le moment du concert arrive et ils sont très contents de voir que beaucoup de gens sont venus les écouter. Ils se présentent, ils jouent, ils chantent... et tout le monde applaudit.

L'entracte arrive et les Anges se reposent un petit moment.
—Ça va bien, hein? dit Robert.
—Oui, c'est formidable, répond Suzanne. Mais je n'ai pas encore vu Michel Henri.

Ils recommencent. Une heure plus tard le concert finit et tous les auditeurs applaudissent très fort.

Mais après, c'est Pierre qui annonce à ses amis la triste nouvelle que Michel Henri, le disc-jockey, n'est pas venu les écouter après tout.

(A SUIVRE)

Un peu de grammaire

More pronouns

In this unit you will have come across a question such as

– Que pensez-vous du dessin?

being answered thus:
– Je **le** déteste!

The word **le** is a pronoun, and is being used to avoid repeating the word **dessin**.
If the question were

– Que pensez-vous de la biologie?

the answer would be:
– Je **la** déteste!

– because, although **le** and **la** both mean 'it', you have to use the one which matches the word it replaces, so for **le dessin** you use **le**, and for **la biologie** you use **la**.

If the verb begins with a vowel, instead of **le** or **la** you use **l'**:

– Je **l'**aime!

– Je **l'**adore!

If you want to use the plural, meaning 'them', this is even easier, because you use **les**, whatever the gender of the noun, thus:

– Que pensez-vous des mathématiques?

– Je ne **les** aime pas beaucoup, mais je **les** préfère au dessin.

Although in these examples **le** and **la** have meant 'it', they are also used to mean 'him' and 'her', e.g.

– Que pensez-vous de Chantal?
– Je **la** déteste!

– Et Marie?

– Je **l'**adore. Tu aimes son frère Pierre?

– Non, je ne **l'**aime pas beaucoup, mais je **le** préfère à Chantal.

Unit 5
Que fais-tu pour t'amuser?

In this unit you will learn how to

– talk about things you and others do in your spare time

– ask about and express opinions on television programmes, films, etc.

– talk about what you and others would like to do

– ask about performance times at the cinema, etc.

– book seats at the cinema, etc.

1 Listen to the cassette. You will hear a number of people being asked about what they like doing in their spare time. As you listen, jot down the activities each of them prefers.

These are the kinds of question you might ask if you want to know what someone else does in their spare time:

Que fais-tu pour t'amuser?

Que fais-tu quand tu es libre?

Comment passes-tu ton temps libre?

Tu as un passe-temps préféré? *hobby*

Quand tu ne travailles pas, qu'est-ce que tu aimes faire?

These questions are all asking virtually the same thing, but you need to be familiar with all the variations. In each case you can answer by using a simple verb, e.g.

Je joue au football.

– but you may, of course, wish to give a much more complicated answer.

2 Practise with a friend asking and answering the questions given in the information box. Now and again, if you feel your friend has not told you enough, you could ask for more, by saying, e.g.

C'est tout?
Et puis?

—or by asking another question, such as

Quelle sorte de livres lis-tu?
Quelle sorte de films vas-tu voir? etc.

3 Listen to the cassette recording in which you will hear a conversation between two girls who are trying to decide how to spend the afternoon, then answer the questions.

1. Why does the first girl think it might be a good idea to go to the cinema?
2. What do they do to find out what's on?
3. What are the two reasons she gives for not going to see *Le Docteur Jivago*?
4. Why wouldn't she be able to understand *Tootsie*?
5. What sort of film is *Jamais Plus Jamais*?
6. What time is it on?
7. Which performance do they decide to go to?
8. What might stop them getting there in time?

4a Look at the advertisement for two cinemas. Answer the questions.

1. Which cinema shows a film at 3 o'clock every day?
2. What is the cartoon called?
3. How old must you be to go and see *A Coups de Crosse*?
4. For which film are there reduced prices?
5. What can you find out by telephoning 47.31.92?

56

4b Look at the advertisement again, then read this passage and answer the question which comes at the end.

Deux jeunes filles, Hélène et Chantal, essaient de décider quel film elles vont voir vendredi soir. Hélène n'a que dix-sept ans. Chantal n'aime pas les dessins animés, et elle n'aime ni Coluche ni Bruno Cremer. Les classes ne terminent qu'à quatre heures, et leurs mères ne leur permettront pas d'aller à la séance de neuf heures. A quel cinéma vont-elles, pour voir quel film, et à quelle heure?

4c Look at the cinema advertisement again and decide which film you would like to go and see, on what day, and at what time. Then ask a partner, in French:

1. which film he/she would like to see;

2. on what day;

3. at what time.

Then discuss which film you will go to see together, and when.

Questions to ask when you want to inquire about what is on at a cinema or theatre, or you want to buy tickets	
Qu'est-ce qu'il y a au Rex? Qu'est-ce qu'on donne au Balzac? Qu'est-ce qu'on joue au théâtre?	*What's on?*
Ça commence à quelle heure?	*What time does it start?*
Ça finit à quelle heure?	*What time does it end?*
C'est combien, à l'orchestre?	*How much is it in the stalls?*
C'est combien au balcon?	*How much is it in the balcony?*
Un orchestre, s'il vous plaît.	*A seat in the stalls, please.*
Deux balcons, s'il vous plaît.	*Two seats upstairs, please.*

4d Write your own cinema advertisement, along similar lines, but showing different films and different times, and also showing prices for the stalls and the balcony. Decide also what time each performance (= la séance) ends.

4e Working with a partner, imagine you are telephoning a cinema. Find out:

1. what is showing;
2. the time the performance starts;
3. the time it ends;
4. how much it costs;
5. then book some seats.

Your partner will answer by referring to the advertisement he/she devised in the previous exercise. When dealing with the booking your partner will want to know:

1. at what time and on what day you want to go;

2. how many seats you want;

3. what your name is.

Now change roles.

5a Look at the results of this newspaper opinion poll showing which television programmes were most popular during the previous week, then say whether the statements are true or false.

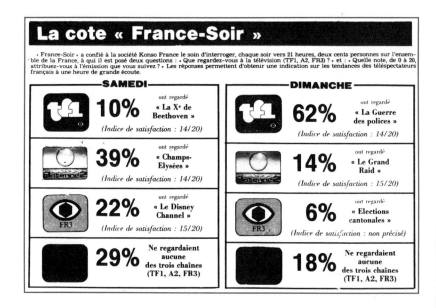

La cote « France-Soir »

• France-Soir • a confié à la société Konso France le soin d'interroger, chaque soir vers 21 heures, deux cents personnes sur l'ensemble de la France, à qui il est posé deux questions : • Que regardez-vous à la télévision (TF1, A2, FR3) ? • et : • Quelle note, de 0 à 20, attribuez-vous à l'émission que vous suivez ? • Les réponses permettent d'obtenir une indication sur les tendances des téléspectateurs français à une heure de grande écoute.

SAMEDI

10% ont regardé « La Xe de Beethoven » (Indice de satisfaction : 14/20)

39% ont regardé « Champs-Elysées » (Indice de satisfaction : 14/20)

22% ont regardé « Le Disney Channel » (Indice de satisfaction : 15/20)

29% Ne regardaient aucune des trois chaînes (TF1, A2, FR3)

DIMANCHE

62% ont regardé « La Guerre des polices » (Indice de satisfaction : 14/20)

14% ont regardé « Le Grand Raid » (Indice de satisfaction : 15/20)

6% ont regardé « Elections cantonales » (Indice de satisfaction : non précisé)

18% Ne regardaient aucune des trois chaînes (TF1, A2, FR3)

1. On a interrogé deux cents téléspectateurs. *Vrai*
2. On a interviewé seulement des gens qui habitent Paris. *Faux*
3. Samedi, la plupart des gens ont regardé «La Xe de Beethoven». *Faux*
4. Samedi, c'est les gens qui ont regardé «Le Disney Channel» qui ont été les plus contents. *Vrai*
5. Dimanche très peu de spectateurs ont regardé FR3. *Vrai*
6. Les gens qui ont vu «Le Grand Raid» ont été moins satisfaits que ceux qui ont regardé «La Guerre des polices». *Faux*
7. Dimanche, il y a eu plus de spectateurs que samedi. *Vrai*

Write out a list of questions that you might ask in French if you carried out the same sort of opinion poll.

5b Carry out an opinion poll yourself by going round the class and asking each of the pupils the questions you have written down.

5c Write up the results of your opinion poll in the same way as it was presented in the newspaper.

Things to say when you are discussing a TV programme, film, etc.

Vous avez vu *Jamais Plus Jamais* au Rex?

Did you
Tu as vu «Dallas» à la télévision?

Tu as entendu «Top 50» à la radio?

Comment avez-vous trouvé *Jamais Plus Jamais*?

Qu'as-tu pensé de «Dallas» hier soir?

Tu as aimé «Top 50»?

C'était formidable (terrible, extraordinaire, magnifique, merveilleux, intéressant, amusant)!
boring   stupid   disgusting
C'était ennuyeux (ridicule, bête, dégoûtant)!

Ce n'était pas bon (terrible, extraordinaire)!

6a Imagine you have been to see a film. Write down which film you saw, who went with you, what you thought of it and why, and what your friend thought of it.

6b Work with a partner. Ask:

1. what film he/she saw;

2. who he/she went with;

3. what he/she thought of the film, and why;

4. what his/her friend thought of the film, and why.

Now change roles.

7 Look at the newspaper cutting showing a selection of television programmes to be shown during the following week, then answer the questions.

TF 1

DIMANCHE 2 SEPTEMBRE línes
18.05 « La Ligne transatlantique », histoire du paquebot « Normandie ».
19.00 « Les Plouffe » (3), feuilleton franco-québécois.
20.35 « L'Hôtel de la plage », film de Michel Lang. Avec Daniel Ceccaldi, Myriam Boyer.

LUNDI 3 SEPTEMBRE
20.35 « Le Gaucher », film d'Arthur Penn. Avec Paul Newman.

MARDI 4 SEPTEMBRE
20.35 « Peter Grimes » opéra de Benjamin Britten. Avec Jon Vickers, Norman Bailey.

MERCREDI 5 SEPTEMBRE
20.35 « Dallas » : « Ray ».
22.00 « Télévision de chambre » : « L'Homme à la valise » téléfilm de Chantal Ackerman.

JEUDI 6 SEPTEMBRE
20.35 « Nana Mouskouri », variétés.
21.35 « L'Enjeu » magazine économique et social.

VENDREDI 7 SEPTEMBRE
20.35 « Salut les Mickey », divertissement. Avec Roger Carel.
22.35 « Marlène Dietrich », document.
23.45 « Les Tympans fêlés », hard rock.

SAMEDI 8 SEPTEMBRE
13.30 « Buck Rogers au XXVᵉ siècle » (n° 10).
17.45 « Aurore et Victorien » (n° 5 et fin).
18.35 « S.O.S. animaux ». Spécial été.
20.35 « Le Vison voyageur » : de Ray Cooney, avec Michel Roux, Jean-Jacques, Annie Jouzier.
22.35 « Alfred Hitchcock présente... » : « Crime parfait ».
23.45 « Fréquence vidéo ».

1. What is the name of the ship which is the subject of a programme?

2. What kind of ship is it?

3. Which two countries collaborated to make « Les Plouffe »?

4. What is the setting of Michel Lang's film?

5. What kind of person is Arthur Penn's film about?

6. What kind of magazine programme is « L'Enjeu »?

7. What film does Alfred Hitchcock present?

8. What kind of programme is Nana Mouskouri appearing in?

8a Look at the page from the French version of the *TV Times*, then write down the expressions which mean:

1. a broadcast; Emission   4. the first episode;

2. a serial;   5. a marriage bureau.

3. on page one of the newspapers;

A2 — Mardi 18 déc.

10.30 A2 Antiope
11.55 : FIN.

12.00 Flash actualités - Météo

12.05 L'académie des neuf

Emission proposée par Jean-Claude Buchez. Présentation : Jean-Pierre Foucault.

Face aux deux candidats : **Micheline Dax, Christine Delaroche, Stone, Daniel Prévost, Jean Lefebvre, Jean-Claude Dauphin.** Chanteuse : **Amélie Morin** : « J' m'ennuie toute seule dans mon tableau ». Invitée : **Patricia Lesieur.** Vedette : **Douchka** : « Un, deux, trois, Mickey, Donald et moi ».

12.45 Antenne 2 midi - Le journal

13.30 LA MARIEE EST TROP BELLE ★★

Feuilleton en 10 épisodes d'après le roman d'Odette Joyeux. Réalisation : Gérard Espinasse.

Ce nouveau feuilleton raconte l'histoire de Chouchou, le mannequin-vedette de « L'amour de vivre », un journal dynamique.

Découverte le jour de ses dix-sept ans par Michel, Chouchou a été immédiatement adoptée par Judith qui la traite comme une belle enfant un peu demeurée.

Souvent à la « une » des journaux, elle fait rêver dans les chaumières puisqu'elle représente, selon son directeur, la mariée dont on rêve mais qui n'existe pas...

PREMIER EPISODE. Le grand journal féminin « L'amour de vivre » prépare un numéro exceptionnel basé sur le mariage de sa cover-girl vedette et de son partenaire. Chouchou et Patrice vont jouer la comédie du bonheur.

Chouchou (Camille de Casabianca), Michel (Philippe Lavot) et Judith (Axelle Abbadie).

AVEC : Chouchou : **Camille de Casabianca** ; Michel : **Philippe Lavot** ; Judith : **Axelle Abbadie** ; Toni : **Boris Bergmann** ; Patrice : **Xavier Florent** ; Raspanti : **Patrice Alexandre** ; Victoire : **Agnès Andersen** ; Santine : **Brigitte Sauvane** ; Yvonne : **Marcelle-Jeanne Bretonnière** ; Commandant : **Harold Kay** ; Commandante : **Béatrice Constantini** ; Fontaines : **Gérard Dauzat** ; Docteur : **Maurice Travail** ; Croche : **Gérard Prost** ; Curé : **Georges Ser** ; Organiste : **Philippe Girard** ; Juliette : **Elsy Clergeau** ; Femme organiste : **Sabine Larivière.**

13.45 Aujourd'hui la vie ★

UN AMOUR DE CHIEN. Le monde des chiens déclenche bien des passions. Agence matrimoniale spécialisée, couturier, parfumeur, astrologue, détective, bijoutier, coiffeur, maroquinier, psychologue, restaurateur, kinésithérapeute, décorateur, tout y est.

Calqué sur notre environnement, l'univers canin s'enrichit chaque jour de nouveaux professionnels et de nouvelles boutiques.

14.50 La légende de James Adams

Série américaine. Réalisation : Jack B. Hively. L'ETRANGER. Grizzly prend des mesures pour arrêter la menace qui pèse sur la faune. AVEC : **Dan Haggerty** (Grizzly Adams), **Denver Pyle** (Mad Jack), **Don Shanks** (Nakomal), **Bozo** (l'ours).

15.40 Le grand raid

Reprise de l'émission diffusée dimanche. 93

8b Look at the TV page again, and answer these questions:

1. At what time can you see the weather forecast?

2. In what programme can you hear a singer singing about being bored on her own?

3. What programme is concerned with the threat to wildlife?

4. What is Chouchou's profession?

5. What is the subject of «Aujourd'hui la vie»?

6. In which programme could you learn about
   (i)   a dog's astrologer?
   (ii) a women's magazine called *Love of Life*?
   (iii) the latest news?

8c Looking at the same day's programmes, and working with a partner:

1. Say which programme you would like to watch.

2. Ask which your friend would like to see, and why.

9   With a partner, practise asking what was on television last night and what he/she thought of what was on.

10a Read this newspaper item, then answer the questions.

L'appareil anti-pub

Heureusement que nos petits écrans français ne sont pas comme ceux des Américains envahis par la publicité! Même si cela nous arrivait un jour, un Américain qui a fabriqué un appareil anti-pub pourrait y remédier.

Celui-ci vient d'inventer une machine qui s'appelle «éliminateur de publicité» et qui se branche entre le téléviseur et le magnétoscope. Chaque fois que le programme change brusquement pour faire place à une publicité, le nouvel appareil évite de l'enregistrer en faisant revenir en arrière la cassette vidéo.

1. What, according to the writer, have American TV screens been invaded by?

2. What is the nationality of the inventor who is mentioned?

3. What is the new device called?

4. Where is it plugged in?

5. When does the device make the video-cassette go backwards?

6. What effect does this have?

10b Look at the newspaper item again, then write down the expressions that mean:

1. our television screens;

2. invaded by commercials;

3. to manufacture;

4. a device;

5. which plugs in to the TV and the video;

6. every time the programme changes suddenly;

7. to record.

 11 Listen to the cassette recording in which you will hear an advertisement from a radio station, then answer the questions.

1. To whom is this advertisement addressed?

2. What are they offering to record for you?

3. Who provides the cassettes?

4. How long would it take?

5. How many programmes can you choose from?

6. How much do you have to pay?

7. Between what dates is the offer open?

12 Listen to the cassette recording in which you will hear another advertisement from a commercial radio station, then say whether the statements are true or false.

1. They are hoping to encourage children to read.

2. You can get the books in your local library.

3. If you want their books, you have to send away for a catalogue.

4. Their books are aimed at teenagers.

5. They have over two hundred titles to choose from.

6. To find out more you have to send 20 francs.

13 Listen to the cassette. You will hear a telephone conversation between a French lady and the presenter of a popular French radio programme. The lady does not know that the conversation is being broadcast. Say whether the statements are true or false.

1. The lady was expecting the call.

2. She thought it was all a practical joke.

3. She guessed what it was about when she heard Jacques Pradel's voice.

4. She had entered a competition.

5. She had won first prize in a competition.

6. She rarely listened to the programme.

7. The winning card in the competition was going to be drawn in half an hour's time.

8. The lady travelled about the world a good deal.

9. She would shortly travel to Réunion.

14 Listen to the cassette recording in which you will hear another item from the same radio programme, then answer the questions.

1. On what days of the week can you hear this programme?

2. At what time does the programme finish?

3. Whereabouts is the adventure playground that Jacques Pradel goes to visit?

4. What had the children built?

5. Where had they put it?

6. How long did it take them to build it?

7. When do they play there?

8. Why don't they spend the night there?

9. What else do they have there?

10. What did they grow in their garden besides lettuce?

11. What did they do with the lettuce they grew?

15 Look at the page from a French magazine, and answer the questions.

LE HIT-PARADE DES
VENTES DE 45 TOURS

Europe1 ET TÉLÉ 7 JOURS

TOUS LES JOURS DE 16 H A 18 H
LE DIMANCHE DE 9 H 15 A 12 H

10.000 F A GAGNER

POUR JOUER
ÉCOUTEZ **Europe1**
ET ENVOYEZ VOTRE
COUPON-RÉPONSE
OU VOTRE CARTE
POSTALE A :
EUROPE 1
TOP 50
CEDEX 1
75400
PARIS BRUNE.

TOP 50 DU 9 AU 15 DÉC.

1. PETER ET SLOANE	BESOIN DE RIEN, ENVIE DE TOI	1
2. STEVIE WONDER	I JUST CALLED TO SAY I LOVE YOU	2
3. RAY PARKER JR	GHOSTBUSTERS	5
4. COOKIE DINGLER	FEMME LIBÉRÉE	7
5. JERMAINE JACKSON & PIA ZADORA	WHEN THE RAIN BEGINS TO FALL	4
6. FRÉDÉRIC FRANÇOIS	MON CŒUR TE DIT JE T'AIME	6
7. TÉLÉPHONE	UN AUTRE MONDE	9
8. SCORPIONS	STILL LOVING YOU	10
9. QUEEN	I WANT TO BREAK FREE	13
10. GEORGE MICHAEL	CARELESS WHISPER	11
11. CHRIS DE BURGH	HIGH ON EMOTION	8
12. BRONSKI BEAT	SMALLTOWN BOY	17
13. CYNDI LAUPER	TIME AFTER TIME	15
14. BONEY M	KALIMBA DE LUNA	35
15. MARLÈNE JOBERT	C'EST UN ÉTERNEL BESOIN D'AMOUR	
	MICKEY, DONALD ET MOI	20
16. DOUCHKA	DÉLIRE D'AMOUR	14
17. MICHEL SARDOU	THE REFLEX	16
18. DURAN DURAN	WAKE ME UP BEFORE YOU GO-GO	21
19. WHAM	WAR SONG	19
20. CULTURE CLUB	DISPARUE	18
21. MADER	WHAT'S LOVE GOT TO DO WITH IT	22
22. TINA TURNER	CARIBBEAN QUEEN	24
23. BILLY OCEAN	TORTURE	27
24. JACKSONS	HELLO	31
25. LIONEL RICHIE	LA FILLE AUX BAS NYLON	30
26. JULIEN CLERC	DREAM	40
27. P. LION	BEAU, J'S'RAI JAMAIS BEAU	32
28. CLAUDE BARZOTTI	AMÉRICAIN	23
29. JEAN-JACQUES GOLDMAN	HONG KONG STAR	12
30. FRANCE GALL	T'AS LE LOOK, COCO	E.
31. LAROCHE-VALMONT	SOUNDS LIKE A MELODY	34
32. ALPHAVILLE	RIEN A PERSONNE	28
33. JOHNNY HALLYDAY	PRECIOUS LITTLE DIAMOND	37
34. FOX THE FOX	BIG IN JAPAN	33
35. ALPHAVILLE	IT'S MY LIFE	36
36. TALK TALK	AGAINST ALL ODDS	26
37. PHIL COLLINS	TOUTE PREMIÈRE FOIS	E.
38. JEANNE MAS	SMOOTH OPERATOR	43
39. SADE	ARRÊTE TON CLIP	49
40. MINI-STAR	ALL OF YOU	E.
41. JULIO IGLESIAS & DIANA ROSS	PHANTASMES	47
42. AXEL BAUER	HIGH ENERGY	39
43. EVELYN THOMAS	TO FRANCE	38
44. MIKE OLDFIELD	WHEN DOVES CRY	E.
45. PRINCE	SUSANNA	46
46. ART COMPANY	LA P'TITE LADY	42
47. VIVIEN SAVAGE	UN JOUR ON SE RENCONTRERA	41
48. LINDA DE SUZA	WOULDN'T IT BE GOOD	45
49. NIK KERSHAW	MASTER AND SERVANT	48
50. DEPECHE MODE	E. entrée cette semaine dans le Top 50	

© EUROPE 1, CANAL +, TÉLÉ 7 JOURS. Tous droits réservés, reproduction même partielle interdite Enquêtes NIELSEN IPSOS • Classement précédent

PRÉNOM :

NOM :

ADRESSE :

TÉL :

Europe1 télé 7 jours

CANAL+

RETROUVEZ TOUS LES SOIRS, DU LUNDI AU VENDREDI,
SUR CANAL +, SANS DECODEUR,
LES VEDETTES DU"TOP 50," DE 20H05 A 20H30.

1. On what days can you hear 'Top 50' in the afternoon?

2. On what day can you hear it in the morning?

3. To enter this competition, on what radio station will you hear the questions you have to answer?

4. If you don't want to cut the coupon out of the magazine, how are you told to send in your entry?

5. On which TV channel can you see a pop music programme?

6. When?

7. Which singer sings a song meaning 'My heart says I love you'?

8. Who sings a song called 'One day we'll meet'?

16 Look at the coupon taken from a magazine, then answer the questions.

1. For what kind of readers do you think this magazine is intended?

2. How long does a subscription last?

3. How often is the magazine published?

4. What five details about yourself do you have to put on the coupon?

5. What do you have to send in besides the coupon?

6. Why are there two different subscription rates?

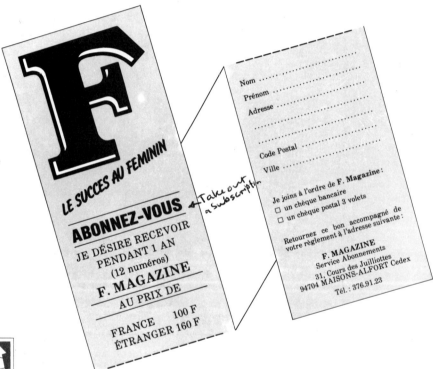

17a Write a short letter to a friend asking:

1. what he/she did yesterday evening (or at the weekend);

2. why;

3. how he/she enjoyed it.

17b Give that letter to a friend, and write a reply to the one your friend gives you in return.

18 Write a letter to a friend saying what you are going to see at the cinema tonight, why you want to go, what other people have said about the film, and asking if your friend has seen it yet.

Un peu de grammaire

Some more pronouns

Look at this conversation:

– Tu as parlé à ton père?
– Oui, je lui ai parlé hier soir. *J spoke to him last night*
– Qu'est-ce qu'il t'a dit?
– Il m'a dit qu'il devrait discuter ça avec ma mère. Eh *wld have to* *had* bien, j'ai demandé ce matin à ma mère si papa lui avait parlé et elle a dit que oui.
– Et ils vont *going* te donner la permission d'y aller?
– Cette fois, non, parce qu'ils n'ont pas assez d'argent. Mais je dois leur demander encore la semaine prochaine.

Here you will see some pronouns taking the place of nouns, as they always do. The pronoun **lui** is taking the place of **à mon père**, but also of **à ma mère**. The pronoun **leur** is taking the place of **à mes parents**. In other words, **lui** is singular and **leur** is plural, but you use the same pronoun for masculine and feminine nouns.

Notice that **lui** and **leur** replace the word **à** as well as the noun.

In the same conversation you will notice the pronouns **me** and **te**. These, along with **nous** and **vous**, are used in exactly the same way as **lui** and **leur**. What is more they can be used in the same way as **le**, **la** and **les** as well. This means that if you want to use a pronoun instead of saying

Je déteste Albert Duval.

you have to say *direct obj-pronoun*

Je **le** déteste.

and instead of saying

Je parle à Albert Duval.

you say

Je **lui** parle.

But you would say

Albert Duval **me** déteste.

and also

Albert Duval **me** parle.

Voici le cinquième épisode de notre feuilleton *Les Anges du Diable*.

C'est le lendemain du concert, à l'heure du déjeuner. Les quatre jeunes artistes bavardent dans la cour. Ils sont très contents du succès de leur concert — après tout, on les a applaudis très fort et on leur a demandé de chanter deux chansons de plus.

Mais ils sont tristes aussi, parce que Michel Henri, le célèbre disc-jockey, n'est pas venu les écouter.
— Vraiment je ne comprends pas, dit Suzanne. Voici sa lettre. Il a bien dit qu'il voulait nous écouter, n'est-ce pas?
— Alors pourquoi n'est-il pas venu? demande Catherine.

— Je voudrais bien savoir, dit Pierre. Mais la question la plus importante, c'est ce que nous allons faire?
— Ha! Ha! Vous ne pouvez rien faire. Michel Henri ne s'intéresse pas à vous, c'est tout! Il s'intéresse aux artistes, pas aux idiots!

Les amis tournent la tête et voient Albert Duval qui les regarde.
— Va t'en, Duval! s'écrie Pierre.

Albert Duval s'en va, riant toujours. Pierre se tourne vers les autres.
— Je me demande, dit-il, si ce Duval n'a pas empêché la visite de Michel Henri.

— Ecoutez! s'écrie soudain Suzanne. J'ai une idée! Nous avons enregistré le concert, non? Alors nous allons envoyer la bande magnétique à Michel Henri!

— Voilà! Bravo! crient les autres.
— Mais qui a la bande? demande Pierre.

Les quatre amis se regardent stupéfaits. Personne n'a la bande! Elle aussi est perdue!

(A SUIVRE)

Unit 6
Faisons les courses...

In this unit you will learn how to

– make comparisons

– ask a shopkeeper if something is in stock

– tell a shopkeeper what you want

– buy goods

1a Look at the advertisement for canned food, then answer the questions.

1. What vegetables are advertised in pictures 1 and 2?

2. What is included with the corned beef?

3. What is in the ravioli?

4. What has been added to the *choucroute*?

5. Has anything been added to the *flageolets verts* and the *thon*?

6. Which is the most expensive product?

7. Which is the cheapest product?

1b Look at the canned food advertisement again, then say whether these statements are true or false:

1. Les petits pois sont plus chers que les pilchards harengs.

2. Le couscous est plus cher que le ravioli.

3. Le cassoulet est plus cher que la choucroute.

4. Les flageolets sont plus chers que le thon.

5. Les flageolets sont le même prix que les harengs.

6. La choucroute est le même prix que les flageolets verts.

7. La macédoine de légumes est moins chère que les haricots verts.

8. Le corned beef est moins cher que le couscous.

9. La choucroute est moins chère que le cassoulet.

If you want to say that something is dear or not, you say, e.g.

Le couscous est cher.
or
Les sardines ne sont pas chères.

If you want to compare the two prices, you say either

Le couscous est plus cher que les sardines.
or
Les sardines sont moins chères que le couscous.

1c Look at the canned food advertisement again, and then write down two different ways to compare the prices of these products:

1. peas/green beans;

2. peas/*macédoine de légumes*;

3. herrings/ravioli;

4. cassoulet/choucroute

5. couscous/herrings;

6. green beans/corned beef;

7. tuna/herrings;

8. *flageolets verts*/peas.

1d Working with a partner, take it in turns, using the lists you have made, and using the canned food advertisement, to ask and answer such questions as:

Qu'est-ce qui est le plus cher, les petits pois ou les flageolets?

Le ravioli est moins cher que les harengs. Est-ce vrai?

Compare le prix du couscous et du thon.

2a Listen to the cassette recording in which you will hear an announcement made in a department store, then answer the questions.

1. In which department will you find the goods mentioned in the announcement?

2. What kind of goods are on offer?

3. For how long are these special offers going to be available?

4. How much are the tins of green beans?

5. What is the most expensive item mentioned?

6. How much is it?

7. What is the cheapest item mentioned?

8. How much is it?

9. What are customers advised to do?

2b Listen to the announcement again, then make up your own announcement, along similar lines, but using different items and different prices. Working with a partner, take it in turns to make your announcement and to write down the answers to these questions:

1. What is the most expensive item mentioned?

2. How much is it?

3. What is the cheapest item mentioned?

4. How much is it?

The easiest way to ask if something is available is to say

Avez-vous...?

e.g. Avez-vous du jambon, s'il vous plaît, madame?

You can ask a little more indirectly, e.g.

Je voudrais du jambon si vous en avez.

If you think they might possibly have sold out of ham, you might ask:

Il vous reste du jambon?

If the shopkeeper has what you want, then there is no problem: you just go ahead and buy it. If what you want is not in stock you may want to know when it will be available, so you might ask:

Vous en aurez plus tard?

Vous en aurez demain?
or
Quand est-ce que vous en aurez?

3 Working with a partner, pretend to be in a grocer's shop. Decide which of you is to be the shopkeeper and which the customer. The customer writes out a shopping list and the shopkeeper writes out a list of what is in stock. The customer then asks if each item is in stock, and the grocer answers accordingly. If something is not in stock the customer asks when it will be available.

Change places so that the shopkeeper becomes the customer and the customer becomes the shopkeeper, then choose a different kind of shop and follow the same procedure.

4a Listen to the cassette. You will hear a man in a baker's shop. As you listen, note down what would have been on his shopping list before he went into the shop.

4b Listen to the conversation in the baker's shop again, and then say whether these statements are true or false:

1. L'homme veut acheter du pain.

2. Il demande quatorze croissants.

3. Il ne reste plus de babas au rhum.

4. La dame lui propose quelque chose d'autre.

5. Il achète quatre éclairs.

6. Il veut commander une tarte pour le weekend.

7. Il commande une tarte aux pommes.

4c Listen to the conversation in the baker's shop again, and then answer the questions.

1. What sort of bread does he want to buy?

2. How many croissants does he ask for?

3. Why doesn't he buy any *babas au rhum*?

4. What does he buy instead?

5. How much does it all come to?

6. Why did he not mention buying a tart before?

7. When does he want it for?

8. What kind of tart does he want?

5 Working with a partner, imagine you want to buy some things from a baker's shop in France. Make a shopping list, then work out how you would ask the following:

1. whether the items you want are available;

2. when the missing items will be available.

Your partner should work out how to say certain things are or are not available, and to say when they will be available. Act out the situation with your partner.

To buy something, you simply say

Je voudrais...

e.g. Je voudrais du jambon, s'il vous plaît.

Or you can say:

Donnez-moi du jambon, s'il vous plaît.

Remember, though, that you usually need to say how much or how many you want, so if you don't make that clear straight away, the shopkeeper will ask you. So decide the quantity you need, and say exactly what you want right at the start, e.g.

Je voudrais quatre tranches de jambon, s'il vous plaît.

Donnez-moi quatre bouteilles de vin rouge, s'il vous plaît.

Je voudrais un kilo de beurre, s'il vous plaît.

6a Listen to the cassette recording in which you will hear a conversation between a shopkeeper and a boy who is shopping for his mother, then answer the questions.

1. What does the shopkeeper think might be the reason for the boy doing the shopping?

2. What is the real reason?

3. How many eggs does he want?

4. How much ham does he need?

5. Why does the shopkeeper ask for his list?

6. How much does the bill come to?

7. What does the boy nearly forget?

6b Listen to the conversation again, and then write out the boy's shopping list.

7 Imagine you are staying with a French family. The parents have sent you to the supermarket and given you a shopping list. Unfortunately it started raining on the way, and part of your list has been smudged by raindrops. Here is your list: rewrite it as it should be.

> 1 kilo de p····es de ter··
> 500 grammes de suc··
> 2 kil·· de tom···
> 4 tra····· de j·mb··
> 2 pa····ts de beu·
> 250 grammes de fro··
> 4 gr·· pa·
> 1 lit·· de la··
> 2 bouteilles de v·· rou··
> 1 bouteille de vi· bl··c

8a Listen to the cassette. You will hear a conversation between a shopkeeper and a customer. Check what the customer asks for against this shopping list, and alter anything that is not the same, so that you have a copy of the list she took with her to the shop.

> 2 kilos de pommes de terre
> 4 kilos de carottes
> 1 kilo de beurre
> 5 kilos de tomates

8b Listen to the conversation again, then answer these questions:

1. Which item is not available at present?

2. Why?

3. When will it be available?

4. What does the customer ask for instead?

5. Why does she want big tomatoes?

6. How much does her bill come to?

7. How much does she give the shopkeeper?

9 Working with a partner, imagine you want to buy some things from a greengrocer's in France. Make a shopping list, then work out how you would do the following:

1. ask whether the items you want are available;

2. ask when the missing items will be available;

3. say you would like to buy the items that are available.

Your partner should work out how to say certain things are or are not available, and to say when they will be available. Act out the situation with your partner.

10 Look at these notices you might see in shops in France. What do they all mean?

EN VENTE AU RAYON LÉGUMES

BOISSONS

CLÔTURE ANNUELLE

CHAUSSURES

VÊTEMENTS HOMMES

LIVRAISON À DOMICILE

PRIX CHOC

CHANGE

PARC DE CHARIOTS

11a Listen to the cassette recording in which you will hear an announcement being made on the public address system of a French village, then answer the questions.

1. Which stall-holder has just arrived at the *champ de foire*?

2. Which others are due to arrive?

3. At what time are they due to come?

4. What is happening tonight?

5. At what time?

6. Where?

7. How much is it to go in?

11b Listen to the announcement again. Imagine that you are staying with a French family, and the mother has asked you to listen out for the announcement and make a note of what it says while she gets ready to go out. Write a note for her in French.

12 Look at the advertisement for a clothes shop in Trégastel, then answer the questions.

BREIZH MOD'

SUPER SOLDE
de rentrée

QUELQUES EXEMPLES

Caban Homme "GRAND LARGUE"	599 F	419 F
Blouson Homme "LE MINOR".	649 F	454 F
Blouson Femme "LE MINOR"	625 F	437 F
Cape "LE MINOR".	735 F	519 F
Jupe de drap "BEAUDOUIN".	325 F	229 F
Véritable Duffle Coat Anglais "GLOVERALL" .	899 F	629 F
Véritable Kilt d'Écosse "RALLY KLAD"	525 F	399 F
Kabig enfant . . . . .le 3 ans	229 F	165 F
le 8 ans	289 F	210 F
Ciré "COTTEN" adulte.	229 F	160 F

Sweater

┌─── PULL MARIN "LE MINOR" ───┐
│ 100 % Woolmark │
│ │
│ Taille 0 à 4 . . . . .l'unité   160 F │
│ les 2   300 F │
│ les 3   420 F │
└──────────────────────────────┘

MANTEAUX - IMPERS - CIRÉS - BOTTES

Offre valable dans la limite des stocks disponibles

TRÉGASTEL
DIRECTION PERROS-GUIREC

1. Why is there a sale at this shop?

2. Name three items of outer clothing that are on sale.

3. What item of clothing is available for both men and women?

4. What price difference is there between the two items?

5. What is priced at 229 francs?

6. What has been reduced from 229 francs to 160 francs?

7. What is made of 100% wool?

8. In what sizes is it available?

9. What is the most expensive item?

13a Listen to the cassette recording in which you will hear two girls discussing what one of them would like to buy, then say whether these statements are true or false:

1. The girl needs something warm for winter.

2. She wants to buy a dress.

3. She prefers bright colours.

4. She only has 160 francs to spend.

5. Size 42 is too big for her.

6. She decides not to try anything on.

13b Listen to the conversation again, then answer these questions:

1. Why does she want to buy something warm?

2. Why is it difficult for her to make a choice?

3. Why does her friend recommend a particular dress?

4. Why does she not try that one on?

5. What does she want to know before she tries something on?

 14a Look at the cartoon, then say whether the statements are true or false.

—Tu vois, ma chérie. On va si bien ensemble. Je viens d'acheter une chemise assortie à ton bras!

1. L'homme a l'air malheureux.

2. L'homme a des fleurs à la main.

3. Il a acheté une chemise neuve.

4. La dame s'est cassé la jambe.

5. Elle est assise dans un fauteuil.

6. La dame porte une robe rayée.

14b Look at the cartoon again, then answer the questions in French.

1. Où est la dame?

2. Pourquoi?

3. Qui est venu la voir?

4. Qu'est-ce qu'il a fait?

5. Qu'est-ce qu'il dit à sa femme?

6. Pourquoi est-ce qu'il sourit?

7. Quelle est la réaction de la femme?

8. Pourquoi?

14c Imagine that your friend has not seen the cartoon, and you want to tell him/her about it. Write down what you would say.

 15a Look at the advertisement, then say whether the statements are true or false.

1. Dans cette boutique vous pourriez acheter une robe du soir.

2. Dans cette fabrique on vous fera une robe sur mesure.

3. Vous n'aurez pas de problème pour garer votre voiture.

4. En décembre la boutique est ouverte tous les jours.

5. Elle est fermée le dimanche matin.

6. On ferme pendant deux heures à midi.

15b Look at the advertisement again, then answer these questions:

1. What sort of shop is this advertising?
2. What building is opposite the shop?
3. Where would you be able to park your car?
4. At what time do they close on a weekday?
5. What are their opening hours on a Sunday?
6. What sort of clothes made of leather could you buy at this shop?

16 Look at the advertisement for wigs, then answer the questions.

SOYEZ BELLE AVEC UNE PERRUQUE

une boutique élégante
un très grand choix
étude personnalisée
ESSAYAGE EN CABINE
(hommes·femmes·enfants)
remboursement Sécurité Sociale possible
renseignements à :

la Maison de la Chevelure

44, RUE DE LONGCHAMP · 75116 PARIS

métro : Trocadéro ☎ (1) **553.28.54**

1. For what customers does the wig shop cater?
2. If you were going there by Underground, where would you get off?
3. How does the advertisement describe the shop?
4. What kind of attention may customers expect?
5. Where can the wigs be tried on?
6. Who may be willing to help the customers pay for a wig?

17 In this conversation between a shopkeeper and a customer the shopkeeper's part is missing. Look carefully at what the customer says, and then write down what the shopkeeper replies.

—Bonjour, monsieur.

—. . . . . .
—Je voudrais une livre de jambon blanc, s'il vous plaît, et puis une livre de jambon de Bayonne.

—. . . . . .
—N'importe. Je prendrai du pâté.

—. . . . . .
—Vous avez du pâté de Strasbourg?

81

Comme ça ?   *Ça soufit ?*

—......
—Non, encore un petit peu, s'il vous plaît. Oui, voilà, comme ça.

is that → *c'est tout ?*
all
autre chose

—......   *stuffed*
—Quatre tomates farcies et quatre artichauts cuits – les plus
gros.   *the biggest*

—......
—Oui, c'est parfait, merci.

18a Listen to the cassette. You will hear the conversation between
the shopkeeper and the customer in full. Check what you
have written down.

18b Listen to the conversation again, then answer the questions.

1. How much cooked ham does the lady ask for?

2. Why does the shopkeeper apologise?

3. What does she have instead of the Bayonne ham?

4. What kind of tomatoes does she ask for?

5. How many cooked artichokes does she want, and what kind?

19 Working with a partner, look at this role-play situation. Decide
which of you will play the part of the shopkeeper and which the
customer, then, working together, decide what the customer
would say and what answers the shopkeeper might give. Act out
the situation.

1. Ask if he/she has any magazines for teenagers.

2. Ask what magazines would be suitable for your mother who
doesn't understand French very well.

3. Find out about prices and ask for something cheaper.

4. Buy the local newspaper.

5. Settle your bill.

20 Imagine that you are going on holiday to France, and will be
staying in a cottage next to a farm. Your parents have asked you
to write to the owners, who live on the farm, to tell them what
food you would like them to leave in the cottage for when you
arrive: namely milk, butter, bread, cheese, potatoes, ham and
tomatoes. Say in your letter that your parents will pay for it all
when you get there.

Un peu de grammaire

The Perfect Tense (Passé Composé)

The Perfect Tense is a *past* tense, but it is not the one you always use when you are talking about something that happened in the past.

When to use it:
You use it where we would use 'I have' with another verb, e.g. 'I have eaten', 'I have been', etc.

You also use it where we would say, for instance, 'I sang', 'I ate', 'I went', etc., *but only if both the following statements are true:*

(i) you are talking about one occasion only;
(ii) you could not change, e.g. 'I ate' to either 'I would eat' or 'I used to eat' without changing the meaning of the sentence.

So this is what you would do in these sentences:

On Friday night I ate three cakes.
> – use Perfect Tense

On Friday nights I always ate fish and chips.
> – do *not* use Perfect Tense

Voici le dernier épisode de notre feuilleton *Les Anges du Diable*.

Une semaine a passé depuis le concert. Les quatre Anges ont cherché partout, mais en vain. On n'arrive pas à trouver la bande perdue.

Tous leurs amis, et beaucoup d'autres personnes aussi, ont dit que leur concert était sensationnel.

Mais pour trouver le véritable succès, les disc-jockeys sont plus importants que les amis. Ils ont décidé que la seule chose à faire, c'est de donner un nouveau concert— seulement il faut attendre trois mois pour pouvoir réserver encore la salle du Café Longchamp.

Robert, Pierre et Catherine bavardent dans la cour. Soudain Suzanne arrive, brandissant un bout de papier.
—Regardez! crie-t-elle. Lisez cette lettre!

Catherine prend la lettre et lit à haute voix.

Chère Suzanne,

Merci pour le coup de téléphone pour me dire que le concert n'allait pas avoir lieu. Ce que je ne comprends pas, c'est que votre père m'a envoyé un enregistrement du concert. N'importe—vous m'expliquerez un de ces jours. Le plus important, c'est que j'ai écouté la bande et que je trouve votre musique fantastique. Voulez-vous me donner la permission de passer quelques chansons à la radio?

Bien à vous,
Michel Henri

Les autres écoutent en silence.

Alors ils crient, ils sautent, ils s'embrassent. Ils sont si contents qu'ils ne se demandent pas encore qui avait téléphoné pour dire que le concert n'aurait pas lieu.

Mais Albert Duval, qui les regarde d'un œil jaloux, pourrait peut-être leur donner la réponse!

(FIN)

Unit 7
Tout le monde à table!

> **In this unit you will learn how to**
>
> – say what you like to eat and drink
>
> – ask what someone else likes to eat and drink
>
> – say what you would like to eat and drink
>
> – ask what others would like to eat and drink

1 Listen to the cassette recording in which you will hear a conversation between a boy and a girl who are discussing what they like drinking, then answer the questions.

1. What two things does the girl like drinking?

2. What two things does the boy like drinking?

2 Working with a partner, take it in turns to ask and answer questions about likes and dislikes, e.g.

Qu'est-ce que tu aimes?

Qu'est-ce que tu aimes faire?

Aimes-tu la bière? etc.

3 Listen to the cassette recording in which you will hear a boy and girl discussing what their parents like to drink, then answer the questions.

1. What kind of wine do the girl's parents usually drink?

2. When does her father drink beer?

3. What does the boy's mother drink before a meal?

4. What does his father have with his Pastis?

4   Working with a partner, take it in turns to ask and answer
    questions like the ones you have just heard on the cassette. Ask
    about each other's parents, family or friends as well as about
    each other.

5   Look at the pictures of four people. Under each picture you will
    find a list of things they like eating, drinking and doing, and
    things they don't like. Work with a partner, and take it in turns
    to ask and answer a question in French, e.g.

    Qui aime les asperges?

    Qu'est-ce que Jean et Marie n'aiment pas faire, etc.

	Marie	Jean	Hélène	Pierre
aime:	asperges	escargots	jambon	escargots
	cognac	vin rouge	vin blanc	vin blanc
	manger	cuisiner	manger et	boire
			boire	
déteste:	œufs	porc	œufs	ratatouille
	vin rouge	limonade	cognac	eau
	faire la	faire la	faire la	manger sans
	vaisselle	vaisselle	cuisine	boire

washing up

6   Look at those people and their likes and dislikes again, then
    write in French as many sentences about them as you can,
    remembering that you can talk about more than one person at a
    time!

When you want to say you like something, simply say, e.g.

J'aime le fromage.

J'aime les œufs.

If you really like it very much, say:

J'aime beaucoup le fromage.
or
J'adore les œufs.

If you want to say you dislike something, say:

Je n'aime pas le café.

And if you really can't stand it, say:

Je déteste le café.

Notice that in all these examples you say *le* **café**, *les* **œufs**, etc.

If you want to say you like or dislike *doing* something, use the same verbs, followed by the infinitive of another verb, e.g.

J'aime manger les bananes.

Je déteste faire la cuisine.

7 Look at each of these sentences, then write another one contradicting it, using the verbs **aimer**, **adorer** and **détester**, e.g.

Marie-France aime les escargots?

Mais non, au contraire, elle les déteste!

1. Tu aimes les escargots?

2. Ton père n'aime pas la bière?

3. Ta sœur déteste le jambon?

4. Ton frère aime le bœuf?

5. Julie adore les légumes?

6. Pierre et Marianne détestent le vin rouge?

7. Marianne et Julie aiment le thé?

8. Toi et ta sœur, vous n'aimez pas les glaces?

8 Read the advertisement for a guide-book, then answer the questions. *To have / just done*

Vient de paraître
LA PETITE BIBLE
des auberges, hôtels, restaurants de la région parisienne

Ouvrage de luxe, format poche, couverture simili cuir vert bronze. 84 pages. Très pratique à utiliser.

58 bonnes tables autour de Paris (de 50 à 100 km) sélectionnés pour leur rapport *mixture* qualité-prix et leur environnement agréable.

Prix : 28 F. En vente dans la plupart des librairies de Paris et région parisienne et drugstores ou chez l'éditeur : « Petite Bible » 41, rue Ibry, 92200 Neuilly-sur-Seine Tél. : 758.12.40.

1. How long has this guide been out?

2. What does it list as well as restaurants?

3. What part of France does it deal with?

4. How far away from Paris is the most distant place mentioned?

5. What two things have been taken into account in the choice of places to recommend?

6. If you can't find it in your local bookshop, where else might you buy it?

7. How big is the book?

8. How much would it cost you?

Je viens de finir mon repas – I have just finished my dinner

9a Look at these advertisements, then rewrite the sentences, filling in the gaps with the name of the appropriate restaurant.

1. Le restaurant qui s'appelle . . . . . . a fêté l'anniversaire de ses cent ans.

2. Le restaurant qui s'appelle . . . . . . est fermé le dimanche et le lundi.

3. Le restaurant qui s'appelle . . . . . . sert des truffes et des pâtes.

4. Le restaurant qui s'appelle . . . . . . a un orchestre.

5. Le restaurant qui s'appelle . . . . . . sert surtout des fruits de mer.

6. Le restaurant qui s'appelle . . . . . . sert un dîner aux chandelles.

9b Look at the restaurant advertisements again, and then answer the questions.

1. On which days can you not go to 'Au Franc Pinot'?

2. What kind of music can you hear at the 'Plateau de Gravelle'?

3. Which two restaurants offer oysters?

4. Where can you eat truffles?

5. What has 'Le Saulnier' to celebrate?

6. What has the 'Taverne Kronenbourg' to offer apart from food?

9c Work with a partner. Look at the restaurant advertisements again, and discuss which restaurant you would like to go to. For example, your partner might say, 'Je voudrais manger des huîtres', so you would say, 'Alors il faut aller à l'Escale'.

Then change roles.

If someone offers you something to eat or drink, and you want to accept, say:

Oui, s'il vous plaît.
or
Oui, je veux bien.
or even
Oh oui, j'adore ça!

If you don't want any, say:

Non, merci.
or
Merci, non.

Be careful not to say just **Merci** if you want something, because that means 'No, thank you'!

10a Look at the two menus, then answer the questions.

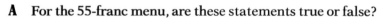

$\mathcal{M}$enu à 55^f	$\mathcal{M}$enu à 90^f
¼ de vin et service compris	Boisson et Service 15% non compris
Potage du jour ou L'Assiette de Cochonaille ou L'Oeuf à la Russe ou Le Colin Mayonnaise et ¼ Poulet Rôti Frites, Petits Pois ou Le Filet de Merlu Panné Pommes vapeur ou La Noix de Porc Rôti Frites, Petits Pois et Fromage ou Fruit ou Glace	Potage du jour ou La Terrine du Chef et Les Moules Marinières ou Les Asperges Savoyardes et La Noix de Porc à l'Orange Frites, Petits Pois ou Le Coquelet au Vin Pommes vapeur, Petits Pois ou La Truite à la crème Pommes vapeur et Fromage ou Fruit ou Glace ou Pâtisserie

A For the 55-franc menu, are these statements true or false?

1. Service is not included.

2. Wine is included.

3. None of the starters includes egg.

4. There is fried chicken on the menu.

5. There are chips with all the main courses.

6. You can have either cheese or another dessert.

B For the 90-franc menu, are these statements true or false?

1. There is no soup.

2. You can have asparagus.

3. Drinks are included in the price.

4. You can have chips with roast pork.

5. You can have peas with chicken.

6. There is no fish offered.

10b Look at the two menus and say which one these statements refer to:

1. You have to pay extra for drinks and service.

2. You could eat mussels as a starter.

3. You would have four courses.

4. You could have chicken with boiled potatoes and peas.

5. You could have trout.

6. You could not choose to have pastry for dessert.

> When you are ordering something in a café or a restaurant, you say
>
> **Je voudrais...** (just as you would in a shop)
>
> But you can also state your intention, e.g.
>
> Je vais prendre un coca-cola, s'il vous plaît.
>
> Je vais manger un bifteck.
>
> Or you can give a direct instruction to the waiter:
>
> Donnez-moi une bouteille de vin rouge, s'il vous plaît.
>
> Apportez-nous deux bières, s'il vous plaît.

11 Listen to the cassette recording in which you will hear a conversation between a woman and a waiter in a café, then answer the questions.

1. What does the lady want to know when she first enters the café?

2. Where does she decide to sit?

3. Why?

4. What does she order for herself and her friend?

12 Listen to the conversation between a man and a waitress in a restaurant, then answer the questions.

1. Where do the man and his companion want to sit?

2. What do they have instead of an apéritif?

3. What does the waitress ask if the man wants to do?

4. Why doesn't he want the *poulet basquaise*?

5. Why does the waitress recommend the *daube de bœuf*?

6. What starters does the man order?

13 Listen to the cassette. You will hear a conversation involving an Englishman who is entertaining a French business colleague at a Paris restaurant. Answer the questions.

1. Why does the first man congratulate the other?

2. Why does the other suggest that he should wait before congratulating him?

3. What does the first man choose for the first course?

4. What does he choose for the second?

5. What vegetables does he choose to go with his veal chops?

6. How many bottles of wine are they going to order?

7. Which course are they going to drink red wine with?

8. What does the first man think of English cooking?

9. What compliment does he pay the French?

10. What is his colleague's reaction?

14 Working with a partner, take it in turns to order a drink, with the waiter or waitress asking

Vous désirez, monsieur/madame?

and the customer choosing something different each time. Make sure you practise all the ways of ordering that have been mentioned in this unit.

15 Work with a partner. Imagine that you are in a French restaurant, and you are each handed the two menus shown on page 92. You should each decide first of all which menu you prefer, and then what you want to eat. Ask

1. which menu your friend has chosen;

2. which dishes he/she has chosen;

3. what he/she would like to drink.

16 Work with a partner. Imagine you are in a French café. Your partner is the waiter/waitress (his/her part in brackets).

1. (Where would you like to sit?)
   Say where you would like to sit.

2. (What would you like to drink?)
   Order drinks for yourself and two other people, each person choosing something different.

Then change roles with your partner.

17 Work with a partner. Imagine you are in a French restaurant, and your partner is the waiter or waitress. Answer the questions asked by the waiter/waitress as well as following these instructions. You should each prepare your role beforehand.

1. Ask for a table for two.

2. Ask what the waiter/waitress recommends.

3. Order a meal for two.

4. Ask the waiter/waitress for some wine.

The waiter/waitress will:

1. ask whereabouts you would like to sit;

2. recommend a dish from the menu;

3. ask if you would like an apéritif;

4. ask what kind of wine you would like.

Then change roles with your partner.

18 Listen to the cassette recording in which you will hear a conversation in the kitchen between a husband and wife, then say whether these statements are true or false:

1. The man is having a pre-dinner drink while his wife does the cooking.

2. The woman is having a pre-dinner drink while her husband does the cooking.

3. The man finds cooking tiring after a day at the office.

4. He asks his wife to pass him a knife.

5. He does not think the vegetables are very good.

6. The woman always buys her vegetables at the market.

7. This year the quality of vegetables is very good.

19 Look at these suggestions for making sandwiches, then answer
the questions.

A Jambon blanc, dégraissé. Rôti de bœuf ou de porc en lamelles
(froides) ou poulet.

B Feuilles de laitue et cerises ou abricots frais. Rondelles de
concombres ou de tomates.

C Lamelles de fromage sec. Fromage blanc mélangé de mayonnaise
et relevé d'herbes.

Mettez votre garniture préférée entre deux tranches de pain de seigle
ou de pain complet.

---

1. In each group of four, choose the filling that is suggested
   above.
   (i)   salmon, chicken, pâté, veal;
   (ii) peaches, cherries, pears, bananas;
   (iii) cucumber, onion, radishes, celery;
   (iv) cheese, eggs, butter, jam.

2. What kinds of meat fillings are suggested?

3. What kinds of fruit fillings are suggested?

4. What kinds of vegetable fillings are suggested?

5. What two kinds of bread are mentioned?

6. What is to be added to the white cheese?

20a Look at this recipe for *bœuf bourguignon*, then at the English
translation which follows, but which contains a number of gaps.
Rewrite the translation, filling in the gaps.

Coupez en morceaux un kilo de bœuf. Faites chauffer du beurre, puis
faites cuire le bœuf, à feu vif, mais pendant quelques instants
seulement, avec quelques oignons et quelques petits morceaux de
lard. Flambez si vous voulez, et saupoudrez de farine. Ajoutez trois
verres de vin rouge et faites bouillir. Ajoutez du poivre, du sel, de l'ail,
et faites cuire à petit feu pendant trois heures. Au tout dernier
moment, ajoutez de petits champignons et saupoudrez de persil
haché.

Cut a kilo of ...... into .... Heat some ......, then cook the
...... over a fast heat, but only .... minutes, with
some ...... and a few little pieces of .... Flambé it if you wish,
and sprinkle with .... Add .... of .... and
bring to the boil. Add ......, ... and ......, and simmer for
.... Right at the end add some little ...... and sprinkle
with chopped ....

20b Imagine you are staying in a French family, and have offered to
prepare *bœuf bourguignon*. Your French friend has offered to
buy the ingredients for you, and needs a shopping list. Write the
list in French of what items you need.

21 While on holiday in France your mother has bought a packet of
chocolate mousse, but does not understand all the instructions.
Look at the instructions, then tell her:

1. what sort of bowl she needs to mix it in;

2. how much milk she needs;

3. how to tell when it has
   been beaten enough;

4. how long she needs to
   keep it in the fridge;
   and how long it will
   keep;

5. what kind of milk she is
   advised to use;

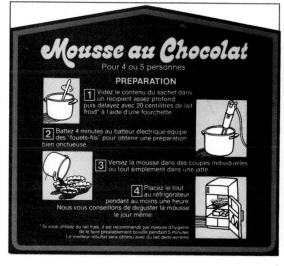

22a Listen to this recipe,
given on the radio, for
ratatouille niçoise. Write
down the ingredients
you need if you want to
make the dish.

22b Listen to the recipe again, then say whether these statements are true or false:

1. It is advisable to use small tomatoes.

2. It does not matter whether you use green or red peppers.

3. Garlic is an essential ingredient.

4. It is better not to use olive oil.

5. It is better to cook the vegetables one at a time if you have time.

6. You have to cook the vegetables on a fierce heat.

7. You add seasoning at the end.

22c Listen to the recipe again, and write down the instructions in English for your mother, who does not understand French.

23 Imagine that last night, the last night of your holiday in France, you went out with your parents for a special meal. When you get home you write to your French pen-friend about it. Write your letter, saying where you went, what you and everyone else had to eat and drink, what you liked and what you didn't like.

Un peu de grammaire

How to form the Perfect Tense

You need another verb to help form the Perfect Tense, and this will always be the Present Tense of either **avoir** or **être**. This verb is known as the 'auxiliary'. You also need a part of the verb which is known as the 'past participle'.

If the verb ends in **-er**, the past participle will sound exactly the same, but will be spelt slightly differently, so the past participle of **chanter** is **chanté**, though the two words sound the same.

If the verb ends in **-ir**, you will nearly always be right if you just take off the last **r**, e.g. **finir** becomes **fini**. This isn't quite good enough to ensure that you'll be right all the time, but there are only one or two others that you can easily learn separately.

If the verb ends in **-re**, check whether it always goes like **attendre**; if it does, then replace the **-re** by **u**, e.g. **attendu**.

Other verbs need to be learned separately; make sure you do learn them – it's very important.

In the examples given below, we are using **chanter** as an example of the **-er** type, **finir** as an example of the **-ir** type, and **attendre** as an example of the regular **-re** type.

chanter	chanté	finir	fini	attendre	attendu
apprendre	appris	avoir	eu	battre	battu
boire	bu	comprendre	compris	conduire	conduit
courir	couru	devenir	devenu	devoir	dû
dire	dit	disparaître	disparu	dormir	dormi
écrire	écrit	être	été	faire	fait
lire	lu	mettre	mis	mourir	mort
obtenir	obtenu	offrir	offert	ouvrir	ouvert
partir	parti	permettre	permis	pouvoir	pu
prendre	pris	promettre	promis	recevoir	reçu
réussir	réussi	revenir	revenu	rire	ri
savoir	su	sentir	senti	servir	servi
sortir	sorti	suivre	suivi	tenir	tenu
venir	venu	voir	vu	vouloir	voulu

Which auxiliary do I use?

Most of the verbs you need use **avoir**, but there are some that use **être**, including some common ones. These are dealt with in the next unit.

Here is an example of two verbs that take **avoir**.

chanter *to sing*	attendre *to wait*
j'ai chanté	j'ai attendu
tu as chanté	tu as attendu
il a chanté	il a attendu
elle a chanté	elle a attendu
nous avons chanté	nous avons attendu
vous avez chanté	vous avez attendu
ils ont chanté	ils ont attendu
elles ont chanté	elles ont attendu

Unit 8
A quelle heure part le train?

In this unit you will learn how to

– find out about arrival and departure times

– find out about changing trains

– ask about prices

– book seats

– buy tickets

 1a Look at the instructions taken from an SNCF (= Société Nationale des Chemins de Fer Français, or French Railways) booklet, and then answer the questions. The number of each question corresponds to the number of the picture.

Comment bien voyager

1. VOUS AVEZ DÉCIDÉ DE PRENDRE LE TRAIN. VOUS CHOISISSEZ VOTRE HORAIRE EN PÉRIODE BLEUE OU BLANCHE, VOUS VOYAGEREZ PLUS CONFORTABLEMENT...

2. ...ET VOUS DISPOSEREZ DE TARIFS RÉDUITS PLUS NOMBREUX.

1. During which periods in the time-table will you travel most comfortably?

2. What other benefits do these periods offer?

3. How can you be sure of obtaining a seat?

4. When should you arrive at the station?

5. Why do you need to look at the main departure board in the station?

6. Why do you need to 'composter' your ticket?

7. What number should you check?

8. Where are the reserved ticket numbers shown?

1b Now look at the instructions again, and answer these questions in French:

1. Qu'est-ce que vous devez consulter avant de voyager?

2. Quel profit y a-t-il à voyager en période bleue ou blanche?

3. Qu'est-ce que vous devriez faire en achetant votre billet?

4. Que ferez-vous pour prendre tranquillement votre train?

5. Comment saurez-vous le numéro de votre quai?

6. Que ferez-vous avant d'accéder au quai?

7. Qu'est-ce que vous chercherez sur le tableau de composition des trains?

8. Qu'est-ce qui est indiqué sur les volants marque-place?

2a Listen to the cassette. You will hear a conversation between a woman and a railway employee in which the woman is asking about times of trains from Bordeaux to Lyon. Answer the questions.

1. What time does the first train the man mentions leave Bordeaux?

2. What time does it arrive in Lyon?

3. Why does the passenger not choose to travel on that train?

4. What time does the second train the man mentions leave Bordeaux?

5. What time does it arrive in Lyon?

6. What appeals to the woman about the second train?

2b Listen to that conversation again, then write down in French the three questions the woman asks the railway employee.

3a Working with a partner, look at this time-table for the Bordeaux–Lyon line. It gives details of the two main trains of the day. Practise asking what time trains leave or arrive, in this way:

A Je suis à Libourne. A quelle heure part le train de Vichy, s'il vous plaît?

B Il part à huit heures sept, monsieur.

A Et à quelle heure arrive-t-il?

B A quatorze heures vingt-six, monsieur.

Then change roles.

Jours de circulation :
TRAIN 4540/1 :
les samedis 27 octobre, 3 novembre, 22 décembre,
le dimanche 30 décembre,
les vendredis du 8 février au 1er mars,
les dimanches 24 et 31 mars, le mardi 9 avril,
le samedi 13 avril.
TRAIN 5440/1 : les dimanches 28 octobre,
4 novembre et 23 décembre, le lundi 31 décembre,
les samedis du 9 février au 2 mars,
les lundis 25 mars et 1er avril, le mercredi 10 avril,
le dimanche 14 avril.

TRAIN 4540/1			TRAIN 5440/1
7 h 45	Bordeaux	▲	20 h 30
8 h 07	Libourne		20 h 07
9 h 05	Périgueux		19 h 09
10 h 06	Brive		18 h 10
10 h 41	Tulle		17 h 34
11 h 57	Ussel		16 h 12
13 h 52	Clermont-Ferrand		14 h 18
14 h 03	Riom		14 h 01
14 h 26	Vichy		13 h 35
15 h 25	Roanne		12 h 28
16 h 44	Lyon Part-Dieu		11 h 13
16 h 54 ▼	Lyon Perrache		11 h 03

3b Look at the Bordeaux–Lyon time-table again, then say whether
these statements are true or false:

1. You can go from Bordeaux to Lyon on Sunday 31 March.

2. You can go from Lyon to Bordeaux on Monday 1 April.

3. The train for Lyon leaves Clermont-Ferrand in the morning.

4. It always takes twelve minutes to travel from one station in
   Lyon to the other.

3c Look at the Bordeaux–Lyon time-table again, then write in
French the answers to these questions:

1. Quels jours de la semaine le train numéro 4540/1 ne circule-t-
   il pas?

2. Combien de lundis le train numéro 5440/1 circule-t-il?

3. A combien de gares le train 4540/1 de Bordeaux s'arrêtera-t-il
   avant d'arriver à Riom?

4. Comment s'appelle la gare qui se trouve entre Tulle et
   Périgueux?

3d Make up your own time-table to show the times of four trains in each direction, on the line from Paris to Valence. (The journey takes just under three hours; do not include any stops between Paris and Valence.)

Working with a partner, ask about departure and arrival times of the various trains, and write them down. When you have done this, compare what you have written with your partner's versions, and then change roles.

4 Listen to the cassette recording in which you will hear a man booking seats and meals on one of the new high speed trains (TGV = trains à grande vitesse), then answer the questions.

1. How many people are travelling?

2. What time do they want to leave?

3. Why does the man need to reserve seats?

4. What class do they want to travel to begin with?

5. What makes the man change his mind?

6. What other reservations does he make?

7. What time will they reach Lyon?

8. What is the man's reaction when he hears the arrival time?

5 Listen to the cassette recording in which you will hear an announcement being made in a railway station, then answer the questions.

1. Who is the announcement meant for?

2. Where has he come from?

3. Where is he being asked to go?

4. Which platform is opposite the place he has to go to?

6 Listen to the cassette recording in which you will hear a man buying a ticket to Chamonix, then answer the questions.

1. What kind of ticket does the man want to buy?

2. How much would it cost him to go second class?

3. How much would it cost him to go first class?

4. Which class does he decide to travel?

Buying a ticket

There are different ways of asking the price of a train ticket. You can say:

Quel est le prix du billet?
or
C'est combien, le billet?
or
Ça fait combien, le billet?
or
Ça coûte combien, le billet?

You also need to say what class you want to travel:

première classe
or
seconde classe

and whether you want a single:

un aller simple

or a return:

un aller-retour.

7   Working with a partner, write down a list of French towns. Then, working alone, alongside each put what you think might be the cost of a railway ticket from Paris. You will need to put four prices, single and return, travelling by both first and second class. (Return will be double the single price.)

Working with your partner again, ask the price of a ticket to one of the towns, making sure that you ask about:

1. a second-class single;

2. a second-class return;

3. a first-class single;

4. a first-class return.

Write down the answers you get, then check against your partner's list, and change roles.

8 Write a short letter to a friend in Rennes. Say that you are going to Rennes on Wednesday 17 April, say what time the train arrives, and ask whether he or she will be able to meet you at the station.

9 Look at these symbols that are used in a railway time-table, then fit the descriptions that follow to the appropriate symbol.

A
D

bar	voiture-restaurant
grill-express	arrivée
départ	vente ambulante
Train à grande vitesse	couchettes
voiture-lits	Intercités
Trans Europ Express	

10a Look at the time-table giving details of the train service between Paris and Italy. Study it carefully, then say whether the statements are true or false.

<table>
<tr><th>ALLER</th><th>TGV 1-2</th><th>1-2</th><th>TGV 1-2</th><th>1-2</th><th>TGV 1-2</th><th>1-2</th><th>1-2</th><th>2 1-2</th><th>1-2</th><th>1-2</th><th>1-2</th><th></th><th></th><th>1-2</th><th>1-2</th><th>1-2</th><th>1-2</th><th>TGV 1-2</th><th>1-2</th><th>TGV 1-2</th><th>1-2</th><th>1-2</th><th>RETOUR</th></tr>
<tr><td></td><td>7 23</td><td>*
9 38
9 47</td><td>10 41</td><td>13 29
(arr.)</td><td>15 00</td><td>**
17 03
17 13</td><td>18 47
21 14</td><td>20 39
23 18</td><td>22 00
0 51</td><td>23 56
3 19
6 00
(arr.)</td><td>6 47
6 56
7 57</td><td colspan="2">Paris-Gare de Lyon
Dijon
Lyon Perrache
Lyon Part Dieu
Culoz</td><td>7 25
4 10</td><td>8 55
5 58
**</td><td>10 07
7 35</td><td>**
13 00
12 51</td><td>15 34
13 20
(dép.)</td><td>16 50
16 41</td><td>19 10
17 00
(dép.)</td><td>23 09
21u16
21u07</td><td>23 11
23 01
22 04</td><td>7 30
3 08
0 05
(dép.)</td></tr>
<tr><td></td><td>10 26
(arr.)
</td><td>11 00
11 15
12 26
14 05
16a20
18b29</td><td>12 34
12 43
13 42
14 01
14 17
15 37
17 30
21a11</td><td></td><td>17 00
(arr.)</td><td></td><td>18 29
19 40
21 30
23 10
0a03</td><td>23 57
1 09
3 01
4 53</td><td>2 08
3 25
5 35
8a35
8 10</td><td>3 33
4 51
7k24
8 55
11a25</td><td>8 16
8 28
9 34
11 23
14a15
15a44</td><td colspan="2">Aix les Bains
Chambéry
Modane
Torino
Milano Centrale
Genova</td><td>1 34
0 30
22k23
20 50</td><td>3 14
2 05
23 59
21 38</td><td>4 52
3 48
1 53
21a50
23 57</td><td>11 33
10 27
8 40
7 00
6a04</td><td>15 30
15 16
12 00
10y15
7a53</td><td>19u41
19u29
18 22
16 35
13v20
13b06</td><td>20 25
(dép.)</td><td>21 48
21 26
20 15
18 05
15a20
15a02</td><td></td></tr>
<tr><td></td><td>21c42</td><td></td><td></td><td></td><td>6e05</td><td>8 25</td><td>12j50</td><td>16j20</td><td></td><td>20c04</td><td colspan="2">Firenze</td><td>16p56</td><td>17j32</td><td>19j25</td><td>1c23</td><td></td><td>4c20</td><td></td><td>9c15</td><td>9c40</td><td></td></tr>
<tr><td></td><td>23b55
2d39</td><td></td><td></td><td></td><td>7a07
10a00
22d43
23d15</td><td>10 05
13f51
22g56
23g23</td><td>13 55
16 52</td><td>18a35
21d45
10d05</td><td></td><td>22a15
0m48
13n08
13n15</td><td colspan="2">Roma Termini
Napoli Centrale
Siracusa
Palermo</td><td>13p55
8q30</td><td>15 45
12 45
20d04
20d15</td><td>18 45
16f00
6g58
6g25</td><td>23a05
20a00
9 23
8 55</td><td></td><td>1s15
22t46
9 23
8 55</td><td></td><td>7b20
3m51
14w42
17m00</td><td>6a40</td><td></td></tr>
</table>

A Train à supplément sur le parcours italien. B Ne prend pas de voyageurs à Modane. C Ne prend pas de voyageurs en couchettes de Paris pour Torino et vice-versa. D Sauf les samedis et les 24, 31 décembre, 7 avril et 26 mai (circule le 16, 23 février, 30 mars et 13 avril). F Sauf les dimanches et les 25 décembre, 1er janvier, 8 avril et 27 mai ; circule le 17, 24 février, 31 mars et 17 avril. a) Changement à Torino. b) Changement à Torino, train à supplément et à réservation obligatoire en 1re classe. c) Pour et de Firenze, changement à Torino et Pisa et vice versa. d) Changement à Roma. e) Circule sauf les dimanches et fêtes, changement à Pisa. f) Napoli, Campi Flegrei, changement à Roma, train à supplément, 1re classe seulement avec réservation obligatoire. g) Changement à Roma, train à supplément, 1re classe seulement avec réservation obligatoire. j) Changement à Pisa. k) Torino-Porta-Susa. m) Changement à Torino et Roma. n) Départ de Roma Tiburtina. p) Changement à Milano, train à supplément. q) Changement à Milano. s) Changement à Roma et Torino, train à supplément, réservation obligatoire seulement en 1re classe. s) Roma-Ostiense, changement à Torino. t) Napoli C. Flegrei, changement à Torino. u) Horaires modifiés certains jours. v) Milano P. Garibaldi, changement à Torino. w) Arrivée à Roma-Tiburtina, avec changement de train à Torino. y) Changement à Torino, train à supplément.

* PIEMONTE   ** LE MONT CENIS   .*. PALATINO   .*. NAPOLI-EXPRESS   .*. STENDHAL

1. Le train qui quitte Paris à sept heures vingt-trois du matin est un TGV.

2. Le train qui quitte Culoz à huit heures moins trois ne s'arrête pas à Chambéry.

3. On peut manger dans le train qui quitte Genova à trois heures deux.

4. Le dernier train du jour qui va de Firenze à Lyon part à neuf heures et quart.

10b Look again at the Paris–Italy time-table, then answer these questions in French:

1. A quelle heure doit-on quitter Chambéry pour arriver à Torino à sept heures vingt-quatre?

2. A quelle gare s'arrête-t-on entre Napoli Centrale et Palermo?

3. Comment s'appelle le train qui quitte Lyon–Perrache à 17h 03 et y arrive à 13h 00?

4. Si vous prenez le train qui quitte Firenze à 17h 32, où faut-il changer?

11 Read the instructions given to travellers by the SNCF about 'le compostage' (making your ticket valid by putting it into a red machine before you go onto the platform), then answer the questions.

UTILISATION

Le jour de votre départ, à l'aller comme au retour, vous devez valider vous-même votre billet en utilisant les composteurs mis à votre disposition dans les gares.

Si votre billet n'a pas été validé, le contrôleur, dans le train, le considérera comme non valable.

Les arrêts en cours de route sont possibles, mais vous devez recomposter votre billet au départ de la gare d'arrêt.
N'oubliez pas de faire annuler immédiatement le compostage de votre billet si, une fois cette formalité accomplie, vous avez "raté" votre train et vous n'êtes plus en mesure de voyager le jour-même.

1. When do the instructions say you need to make your ticket valid?

2. Where will you find the machines to do this?

3. Who will check up on this in the train?

4. If you break your journey, what must you do before you get on another train?

5. Under what circumstances should you cancel the 'compostage'?

12a A woman is asking about trains from Paris to Milan, but what she says has been left out. Write down what you think she says.

— ......
— A onze heures vingt-deux, madame.

— ......
— Oui, il faut changer à Dijon, madame.

— ......
— Le prochain train part à quatorze heures treize, madame.

— ......
— Non, c'est direct.

— ......
— A vingt-deux heures trente.

— ......
— Du quai numéro deux.

— ......
— Je vous en prie, madame.

12b Listen to the cassette. You will hear the conversation in full. Check what you have written against what you hear on the cassette, then answer these questions:

1. At what time do the two trains to Milan leave?

2. On which one do you have to change?

3. Where do you have to change?

4. What is the second train's arrival time at Milan?

5. What platform does it leave from?

12c Write down what you would need to ask if you wanted to know:

1. if you need to change trains to get to Annecy;

2. what time your connection is at St Gervais;

3. what time you will arrive in Annecy;

4. what platform the train leaves from.

13 Imagine you are on holiday near Brive. Write a short letter to a friend who lives in Bordeaux and who wants to visit you. Say:

1. what time the train leaves;

2. what time it arrives;

3. that he/she will be able to eat in the train;

4. that it is necessary to change at Périgueux;

5. that you will come and meet him/her at Brive station.

Un peu de grammaire

These verbs take **être** in the Perfect Tense: verbs of coming, staying and going.

Going	*Staying*	*Coming*
aller *to go*	rester *to remain*	venir *to come*
partir *to go away*		revenir *to come back*
entrer *to go in*		retourner *to return*
sortir *to go out*		arriver *to arrive*
monter *to go up*		
descendre *to go down*		
rentrer *to go home*		
mourir *to die*		
tomber *to fall*		

Note: some of the verbs listed as 'going' verbs could also be listed as 'coming' verbs, e.g. **entrer** *to come in* or *to go in*.

All reflexive verbs, e.g. **se lever**, **se laver**, **s'asseoir**, also take **être**.

aller *to go*	s'asseoir *to sit down*
je suis allé(e)	je me suis assis(e)
tu es allé(e)	tu t'es assis(e)
il est allé	il s'est assis
elle est allée	elle s'est assise
nous sommes allé(e)s	nous nous sommes assis(es)
vous êtes allé(e)(s)	vous vous êtes assis(e)(s)
ils sont allés	ils se sont assis
elles sont allées	elles se sont assises

Note that with the **être** verbs, the past participle agrees with the subject. (You will find later that there are some exceptions to this, but it is better for now to stick to this rule.)

In order to make it negative, ignore the past participle and make the auxiliary negative. For example, you would normally say **je n'ai pas** or **vous n'êtes pas**, so you would also say **je n'ai pas dormi** or **il n'est pas parti** or **tu ne t'es pas assis**.

Voici le premier épisode d'une histoire intitulée *Un Voyage en Chemin de Fer.*

— Encore une heure et nous arrivons à Marseille, se dit Marie-France qui commence à s'ennuyer.

Elle jette un coup d'œil sur les autres voyageurs dans le compartiment.

Il y a le vieux monsieur qui dort dans le coin et la grosse femme en face de lui qui tricote à côté du jeune homme qui sourit vaguement de temps en temps en lisant son livre de poche.

Personne ne veut parler à Marie-France qui pousse un soupir et sort son journal illustré de son sac.

Elle est sur le point de lire la
première page quand elle entend une
sonnerie aiguë et le train s'arrête
dans un grincement de freins.

— Qu'est-ce qui se passe? s'écrie la
grosse femme.
— Quelqu'un a dû tirer sur la
sonnette d'alarme, répond Marie-
France. Il doit y avoir un accident ou
bien quelqu'un est malade ou mort.

A ce moment-là on entend des pas
précipités dans le couloir. La
portière s'ouvre, le contrôleur entre
et dit:
— Descendez tout de suite du train!

— Ça doit être grave, pense Marie-
France en se précipitant vers le
couloir avec les autres voyageurs.

(A SUIVRE)

Unit 9
Vive les vacances!

In this unit you will learn

– how to arrange holiday accommodation

– how to tell people about a place you like or dislike and say why

– how to tell other people where you have been or are going on holiday

– how to ask others about holidays

 1a Read this letter written by an Englishman to the *Syndicat d'Initiative* at La Rochelle, then answer the questions.

Chesterton, le 2 février

M.Keith Simpson,
84 High Street,
Chesterton,
Angleterre.

Monsieur le Secrétaire,
Syndicat d'Initiative,
Place Verdun,
17000 La Rochelle,
France.

Monsieur,

J'espère passer une quinzaine [fortnight] à faire du camping en France cet été, de préférence dans une région que je ne connais pas déjà, comme la vôtre. Voulez-vous me donner des renseignements, s'il vous plaît, sur les campings de votre région, et surtout sur l'Ile de Ré.

Je voudrais des renseignements aussi sur les attractions de la région, surtout sur ce qui peut intéresser les enfants, car nous avons deux enfants de six et de sept ans.

Veuillez agréer [Please accept], Monsieur, l'expression de mes sentiments distingués.

Keith Simpson

---

1. How long does Mr Simpson want to spend in France?

2. What kind of a region does he hope to visit?

3. What particular place in the region interests him most?

4. What information does he request about the region?

1b Look again at Mr Simpson's letter, then write down which expression means:

1. I hope to spend a fortnight camping;

2. preferably;

3. will you give me some information, please; *renseignements*

4. what there is to see in the region;

5. to interest the children.

1c Write a similar letter to the *Syndicat d'Initiative* of another French town, asking for information about hotels, restaurants, and interesting places to visit.

2 Read the extract from a brochure on the Ile de Ré such as Mr Simpson might very well have received in reply to his letter, then answer the questions.

Venez dans l'île de Ré...

Séjourner dans l'Ile de Ré, en toute saison, c'est donc vivre pleinement la mer et la nature. Au printemps, vous bénéficierez de son calme et de sa douceur, en été de son éclat et de sa chaleur, en automne de ses tons pénétrants. *colours*

Venez de toute façon, faire provision de santé à l'Ile de Ré, à Ré la Blanche. *warmth/heat*

---

1. What can be enjoyed in the Ile de Ré at any time of the year?

2. Which season of the year is not mentioned?

3. Suggest a reason why the island is called 'Ré la Blanche'.

3 Look at the details of these three hotels on the Ile de Ré. Imagine you are looking for a hotel near the beach, with its own swimming-pool, and own restaurant where you can eat every night. You would prefer somewhere quiet, with good sporting facilities. Which one would you choose?

Centre Bien-Etre et Santé
MAPOTEL - ATALANTE
***NN ⑫

Le Port Notre Dame
17740 STE MARIE
Tél. (46) 30 22 44

A	🛏 65	X	
B	05/02 T.A. 05/01		
C	M. et Mme VERGNON		

Hôtel bord de mer. Restaurant panoramique avec vue sur l'océan. Piscine. Institut de Thalassothérapie à 150 m. Chambres équipées avec téléphone, radio, musique enregistrée, télévision, mini-bar. Salon, solarium, boutique. 10 chambres pour handicapés. 2 tennis. Mini-golf.

HOTEL
LES GOLLANDIERES
**NN ⑬

17580 LE BOIS PLAGE
Tél. (46) 09 23 99
et 09 27 33

A	🛏 32	X	
B	15/12 ↔ 15/11		
C	M Mme FAUCHER		

Situé à 50 mètres de la plage dans un parc d'un hectare. Hôtel, Bar, Restaurant, Discothèque, Piscine. Fermé de mi-novembre à mi-décembre.

HOTEL
LES COLONNES **NN ⑮

19, quai Job Foran
17410 ST MARTIN
Tél. (46) 09 21 58
Rest. fermé le mercredi

A	🛏 29	X	
B	Fermé du 15/12 au 01/02		
C	M. COCHARD		

Hôtel situé sur le port de Saint Martin. Vaste terrasse.

4a Listen to the cassette. You will hear a telephone conversation between a hotel receptionist and a man who wants to book accommodation. Find out:

1. how long he wants to stay;

2. how many people he is booking for;

3. what rooms he requires, and with what facilities;

4. how much the rooms cost;

5. how much breakfast costs.

4b Listen to the telephone conversation again, and write down the expressions which mean:

(handwritten notes to the right:)
(twin)
a deux lit
un grand lit
(double)

1. Do you have any rooms free?
2. How long do you want to stay here?
3. How many rooms do you require?
4. Do you want rooms with bathroom or shower? *(handwritten: douche)*
5. Is breakfast included in the price?

5a Listen to the cassette. You will hear a conversation between a hotel receptionist and a man who has just arrived. Find out the following information:

1. what error has been made;
2. the number of the man's room;
3. what he will have for breakfast the next day;
4. what time he wants breakfast.

5b Listen to the conversation again, then say whether these statements are true or false:

1. M. Massin had not made a reservation.
2. His secretary had telephoned the hotel.
3. His secretary should have confirmed the booking by letter, but didn't.
4. M. Massin had received a letter from the hotel.
5. M. Massin's letter had been filed in the wrong place.
6. M. Massin wanted to leave early the following morning.
7. He had to carry his own luggage to his room.

6 Working with a partner, imagine that one of you is a hotel receptionist, and the other someone requiring accommodation. Act out this situation, with the receptionist asking the questions, then change roles.

1. How many rooms do you want?
2. What sort of rooms do you want?
3. How long do you want to stay?
4. What time do you want breakfast?
5. What do you want for breakfast?

7 Write a letter to the Hôtel les Colonnes at Saint-Martin to book accommodation for yourself and your family. Remember to state:

1. when you want to arrive;

2. how long you want to stay;

3. what sort of rooms you want.

Find out:

4. the price of rooms;

5. the price of breakfast;

6. if the hotel has a restaurant.

8a Listen to the cassette. You will hear a lady arranging to stay at a campsite. Find out:

1. which spot on the site she chooses;

2. for whom;

3. for what vehicles;

4. for how long.

8b Listen to the conversation again, then write down the expressions that mean:

1. Do you have a site? emplacement

2. How many nights do you want to stay here? passer

3. I only have two sites left.

4. Alongside the toilet block.

5. Do you have any children with you?

c'est
décontracté
it is
relaxing.

9 Listen to the cassette. You will hear two young men discussing holidays. When you have heard their discussion, write down:

1. what they think are the disadvantages of staying in hotels;

2. what they think are the advantages of camping;

3. what they think are the disadvantages of camping.

paresseux - lazy (m)
paresseuse lazy (f)

10 Look at the details given about the campsite 'Les Cigales' and then answer the questions.

Le camping international «Les Cigales» ***NN propose 12 hectares de forêt de pins maritimes aux campeurs et aux caravaniers recherchant la nature et le calme.
—à 250 m de la plage
—à 4 minutes du centre commercial (en ville) *relaxation*
Venez y trouver le calme, le repos et la détenté que vous recherchez.
(Ouvert du ler juin au 30 septembre) *walks/rambles*
Distractions: cinéma, dancing, pêche, chasse, voile, sports nautiques, randonnées pédestres. Tennis, échecs, pétanque.
Visite des parcs à huîtres. Plage des enfants par excellence.

1st

1. What is 250 metres from the campsite?

2. How long does it take to reach the shops?

3. When is the camp open?

4. For whom is the beach ideally suited?

5. Which of the following does the campsite have?
   (i) fishing (ii) fencing (iii) volleyball (iv) sailing (v) chess.

6. What can be visited?

117

11a Imagine you want to go camping with your family in France. Write down in French:

1. how many there are in your party;

2. how long you want to stay;

3. where you want the campsite to be;

4. how big a campsite you would like;

5. what facilities you would like there to be at the campsite.

11b Working with a partner, imagine that you have just arrived in a French town and are at the *Syndicat d'Initiative*. Find out from the employee, played by your partner, whether there is a campsite that will correspond to what you have written down. Your partner will pretend that the only campsite in the area corresponds to what he/she has written down, and will answer your questions accordingly. When you have finished, change roles.

12 Working with a partner, imagine that you have just arrived at a French campsite and want to make some enquiries. You should each prepare this separately, then act the situation out together. When you have finished, change roles.

1. Ask if there is a plot free.

2. Ask how much it is.

3. Find out what facilities there are at the site.

4. Find out what there is to do in the area.

Your partner will reply as follows:

1. Ask how many there are in your party.

2. Ask how long you want to stay.

3. Tell you what facilities there are.

4. Tell you what there is to do in the area.

13a Listen to the cassette. You will hear two girls discussing a different kind of holiday, at Tignes. Write down what we are told about Tignes, and what Monique prefers to do.

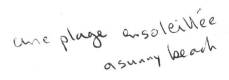

une plage ensoleillée
a sunny beach

13b Look at this extract from a ski-resort brochure, then answer the questions.

[handwritten: nice] *[handwritten: flooded with]*

[handwritten: sun] Fatigué de skier, vous trouverez notre restaurant sympa et sa terrasse inondée de soleil. En fin d'après-midi vous pouvez consacrer votre temps au shopping. Le soir, *[handwritten: devote]* les restaurants puis le bowling, les pianos bar, ou les boîtes de nuit vous laissent l'embarras du choix. *[handwritten: nightclubs.]*

[handwritten: spoilt]

1. When will you particularly enjoy the facilities described here?
2. What is flooded with sunshine?
3. What can you do late in the afternoon?
4. What sport can you enjoy in the evening?

TIGNES vit après le ski

14 Listen to the cassette. You will hear a conversation between two men talking about a holiday one of them has had in the Auvergne. Find out:

[handwritten: alors de quoi te plains tu — what are you complaining about.]

1. what he liked about the region;
2. what he did in the evening;
3. what entertainment there was in the towns;
4. what he chose not to do.

[handwritten: surtout - especially]

15 Listen to the cassette. You will hear one boy explaining to another why he didn't altogether enjoy his holiday in the Pas-de-Calais. Note down his reasons.

 16 Working with a partner, tell him/her, in French, about:

(i) somewhere you have been on holiday;
(ii) somewhere you are going on holiday.

In each case mention:

1. who you went/are going with;

2. how long you stayed/will stay;

3. what there is to do there;

4. what sort of place you stayed/will be staying in;

5. what was good/bad about it or what you hope will be good about it.

Then change roles.

 17a Read the extract from a brochure on Boulogne-sur-Mer. Write down the expressions which mean:

1. a town with fifty thousand inhabitants;

2. sea food;   6. by the sea;

3. a seaside resort;   7. fishing;

4. a beach of fine sand;   8. sailing;   *plaisance*

5. a jolly town;   9. cross-channel sailing.

BOULOGNE-SUR-MER est une ville de 50.000 habitants qui a l'avantage d'offrir à ses visiteurs le triple aspect :

1 d'une capitale gastronomique avec ses spécialités des produits de la mer (poissons - crustacés).

2 d'une ville d'Art et d'Histoire

3 d'une station balnéaire *seaside resort* avec sa plage de sable fin et ses activités nautiques.

Ville souriante, en bordure de mer, les activités de la pêche, de la plaisance, du transmanche, de son port lui assurent une animation appréciée des touristes.

17b Look at the details of Boulogne-sur-Mer again, then answer these questions in French:

1. Combien de personnes habitent Boulogne-sur-Mer?

2. Quelles sont les spécialités gastronomiques?

3. Comment est la plage?

4. Quelles activités y a-t-il sur la mer?

18 Write a letter to a French friend inviting him/her to go on holiday with you, saying:

1. where you hope to go;

2. when and for how long;

3. what there is to do there.

19 Can you solve this holiday puzzle?

Sur la plage de Sainte-Marie, Annette, Babette et **Claudette** passent des moments ensoleillés. L'une d'elles joue à la balle, une autre apprend à nager près du rivage, la troisième fait des pâtés. La pâtissière est fille unique. Babette, qui est la sœur de Claudette, est plus âgée que la nageuse.

What is each one doing?

20 Read this holiday joke, then answer the questions.

A la cuisine une bouteille de champagne et un pot de moutarde sont en train de bavarder. gossiping
— Tu sais, dit le champagne, moi, pour les vacances, je vais sur la Côte d'Azur.
— Tant mieux pour toi, répond la moutarde.
Malheureusement moi, je vais sur la côte de porc.
La côte de porc, qui les écoute, réfléchit tristement qu'elle va bientôt se bronzer — sur un feu de bois!

1. Who is the conversation between?

2. What are they talking about?

3. What is the difference between 'la Côte d'Azur' and *une côte de porc*?

4. What does *se bronzer* normally mean?

5. What has the barbecue to do with it?

21 Look at the map of the Ile de Ré as it is today, then say whether the statements are true or false.

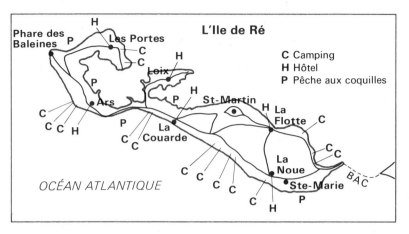

L'Ile de Ré

Phare des Baleines
Les Portes
Loix
Ars
St-Martin
La Flotte
La Couarde
La Noue
Ste-Marie
BAC
OCÉAN ATLANTIQUE

C Camping
H Hôtel
P Pêche aux coquilles

1. On peut pêcher des moules à l'Ile de Ré.

2. Il n'y a pas d'hôtels sur l'Ile de Ré.

3. On arrive sur l'Ile en traversant un pont.

4. La Phare des Baleines se trouve à La Flotte.

5. Il y a des campings à Loix.

22a Listen to the cassette. You will hear two old men talking about the Ile de Ré as it used to be. Find out:

1. what sport the old man used to practise there;

2. where he stayed;

3. how far away the nearest village was;

4. what he did on Saturday evenings.

22b Listen again to the old men's conversation, then answer the questions.

1. Whereabouts are the two men sitting as they talk?

2. What are they drinking?

3. When did Georges used to go to the Ile de Ré?

4. Why wasn't what he did dangerous?

5. What were the local girls like?

6. What does he think of the changes that have taken place?

22c Listen again to the conversation, then write down the expressions that mean:

1. I'd love to!
2. Two more glasses of red wine, please;
3. a short while ago;
4. when you were young;
5. to go sailing;
6. Did you stay at a hotel?
7. not for the better;
8. the good old days.

23 Listen to the cassette. You will hear a conversation between two girls. One of them overheard the conversation between the two old men, and is telling her friend about it. Listen carefully, then answer the questions.

1. What does the first girl want to know?
2. How long does she think it was since the old man last went to the Ile de Ré?
3. What does she think there was on the island at that time?
4. What is there now?
5. What sort of time does she think the old man had there?

24 Think about a place you used to go to on holiday, then give answers, in French, to these questions:

1. Where did you used to go on holiday?
2. How old were you when you went there?
3. Where did you stay?
4. How did you spend the days?
5. What did your parents do during the day?
6. What was there to do in the evenings?

Voici le deuxième épisode d'*Un Voyage en Chemin de Fer*.

Pendant que Marie-France et les autres voyageurs descendent précipitamment du train, le mécanicien et le chef de train suivent un gros homme dans un compartiment de première classe.

—Voilà, dit celui-ci en indiquant du doigt un paquet qui se trouve sous une des banquettes. N'y touchez pas, mais écoutez bien.

Tous les trois entendent un «tic-tac» régulier.
—Mon Dieu! ça doit être une bombe! s'écrie le chef de train.

—C'est fort probable, dit le gros homme. Il faut tout de suite avertir la police pour essayer d'empêcher une explosion.

—Sortons d'ici! dit le chef de train tout pâle.

Les trois hommes rejoignent les passagers qui attendent impatiemment dans un champ près de la voie.

Le mécanicien explique ce qui se passe tandis que le chef de train court à toutes jambes vers la maison la plus proche.

Marie-France commence à avoir peur.
—Est-ce que la police arrivera à temps pour désamorcer cette bombe, ou est-ce qu'elle va éclater? se dit-elle.

(A SUIVRE)

Un peu de grammaire

The Imperfect Tense

The Imperfect Tense is very easy to form. Take the stem of the **nous** form of the Present Tense, (i.e. remove the **-ons** ending), and add these endings:
-ais
-ais
-ait
-ions
-iez
-aient

Examples: chanter – je chantais, etc.
choisir – je choisissais, etc.
vendre – je vendais, etc.
avoir – j'avais, etc.

The only exception is **être**, to which you add those endings to the stem **ét-**, e.g. **j'étais**, **tu étais**, etc.

The Imperfect Tense is used:

1. to describe something or someone in the past, e.g.

   Le monsieur avait les cheveux gris et il portait une barbe.
   Il y a cinquante ans l'Ile de Ré n'avait pas de campings.

2. when an action occurred several times in the past, e.g.
   Le vieil homme allait toujours à l'Ile de Ré où il faisait de la voile.

3. when one action was going on at the time something else happened, e.g.

   Il parlait de ses vacances quand la jeune fille l'a entendu.
   Il faisait du ski quand il s'est cassé la jambe.

Unit 10
Vaut le détour

In this unit you will learn how to

– say how long you are staying in the town/area

– say what you are interested in seeing

– ask for and read printed information – maps, brochures, etc.

– talk about future and past excursions, etc.

The French rarely talk about *staying* in an area as we do; they usually talk about *spending time* there, and the verb to use for that is **passer**, e.g.

Je passe une quinzaine ici.

J'ai passé dix jours à Paris.

If you really want to use the verb 'to stay', use **séjourner**, e.g.

Je séjourne chez mon oncle.

or, in the case of a hotel, **descendre**, e.g.

Nous sommes descendus à un bon hôtel.

The one verb *not* to use is **rester**, because, although you may have learned that **rester** means 'to stay', it really means 'to remain', so if you say, 'Je vais rester chez toi', it means 'I'm going to stay at your house and never leave it'!

127

1a Look at this table, then make up as many different sentences as you can, using one item from each box in the table, to say how long you (or someone else) will be staying somewhere.

Je vais passer	une journée	à La Baule.
Mon frère va passer	quelques jours	en Espagne.
Nous allons passer	une semaine	sur la côte.
Mes amis vont passer	quinze jours	dans le Midi.

To help you make more sentences still, here are some more places you might add to those which appear in the last column of the table:

Royan	en Auvergne	au bord de la mer
Biarritz	en Bretagne	dans la montagne
Cannes	en Suisse	à la campagne
Argelès	aux Etats-Unis	chez mon oncle

1b Working with a partner, take it in turns to ask **Combien de temps vas-tu passer à ... ?**, changing the name of the place and changing the answer each time.

1c Following the same pattern, write ten sentences in French, saying how long these people are going to stay in the place mentioned, e.g.

Je—deux heures au musée.
Je vais passer deux heures au musée.

1. Tu—deux nuits à l'hôtel.

2. Mon frère—une semaine au camping.

3. Ma sœur—trois semaines au Club Méditerranée.

4. Mes parents—un mois sur la Côte d'Azur.

5. Mes deux sœurs—deux jours à Orléans.

6. Vous—deux ans à l'étranger.

7. Nous—une heure au château.

8. Je—quinze jours au bord de la mer.

9. Mon amie—huit jours à la ferme de son oncle.

10. Ils—cinq minutes au Syndicat d'Initiative.

2   Listen to the cassette. You will hear two men talking about holidays in La Baule in Brittany. Now say:

1. who is accompanying the second man on holiday;

2. what he answers when asked how long he is staying there;

3. what he has been told about La Baule;

4. what three sporting activities are mentioned;

5. what his daughter would like to do;

6. what there is to do in the evening;

7. where the man will go if the weather is not very warm.

Notice the different ways of saying that something interests you:

Je m'intéresse aux antiquités.

Ça m'intéresserait d'aller à Montmartre.

J'aimerais bien faire un tour.

Je voudrais aller au Marché aux Puces.

C'est si intéressant de voir les bâtiments.

Don't make the common mistake of thinking that **intéressant** means 'interested' – it doesn't. It means 'interesting', and there is a lot of difference!

3a   Listen to the cassette. You will hear a conversation between a man and woman about what they are going to do during their stay in Paris. Listen carefully, then answer the questions.

1. Why does the woman prefer not to go to the Louvre?

2. Why does she want to go to the Place du Tertre?

3. Which café would she choose in the Place du Tertre?

4. What kind of goods might they buy at the *Marché aux Puces*?

5. What does the man think they might find there?

6. Why is the woman a bit less enthusiastic about it?

7. What would the man like to do tomorrow?

8. What would he find interesting about that?

3b Listen to the conversation again, then write down all the different ways in which the man and the woman said something was interesting.

 4 Imagine that you are in Paris, and think of as many ways as possible of saying you are interested in seeing:

la Tour Eiffel	l'Arc de Triomphe	les Jardins du Luxembourg
le Musée Grévin	le Panthéon	le Quartier Latin
la Conciergerie	la Sainte-Chapelle	le Centre Beaubourg

 5a Look at the time-table for boat trips on the Seine in Paris, then say whether the statements are true or false.

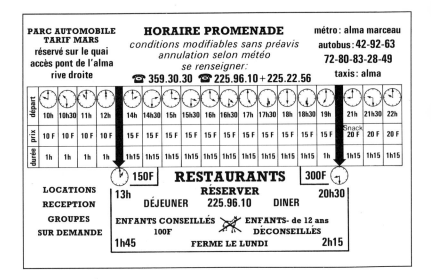

1. Pour faire une excursion en bateau il faut aller au Pont de l'Alma.

2. Cet horaire est pour le mois de mars.

3. Il faut payer plus cher le matin.

4. Le matin les promenades sont plus courtes.

5. Il y a vingt promenades par jour.

6. Il vaut mieux ne pas amener un petit enfant sur le bateau qui part à huit heures et demie du soir.

7. Le lundi on ne peut ni déjeuner ni dîner en bateau.

8. On n'accepte pas les chiens.

5b Look at the boat time-table again, then answer these questions:

1. To which month does this time-table refer?

2. What public transport will take you to the boats?

3. What meals can be eaten on board?

4. Which day are the restaurants closed?

5. When are the shortest trips?

6. When are the most expensive trips?

7. Which bridge will take you to the car park?

8. Why might a trip be cancelled?

9. What does it say about children under 12?

10. How long does the longest trip last?

6a Look at the map of the Seine showing the route taken by a pleasure boat, then write the answers, in French, to the questions.

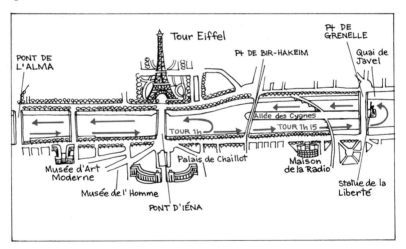

1. Quand on fait la promenade qui dure une heure, sous combien de ponts est-ce qu'on passe?

2. Et quand on fait la promenade qui dure une heure et quart?

3. Quel bâtiment se trouve en face de la Tour Eiffel?

4. Quelle statue se tient au milieu de la Seine?

5. Quand on arrive au Quai de Javel, que fait le bateau?

6. Devant quel bâtiment passe-t-on juste avant le Quai de Javel?

7. Où se trouve l'Allée des Cygnes?

6b Imagine that you have just been on a boat trip along the Seine, and write in French a short account of your trip for your school magazine. Say:

1. what time you started;

2. how long it lasted;

3. what the weather was like;

4. what you saw on your right and left;

5. whether you passed under any bridges.

7a Look at the details about the services offered by the *Syndicat d'Initiative* at Tours, then say whether the statements are true or false.

OFFICE DE TOURISME de TOURS

SYNDICAT D'INITIATIVE DE TOURAINE
Bureau de la Chaîne Nationale d'Accueil et d'Information

 05.58.08

Télex 750008

ACCUEIL DE FRANCE

Place de la Gare 37042 TOURS Cedex

Photo ARSICAUD

ACCUEIL
L'office de Tourisme de TOURS a actuellement six hôtesses. Elles parlent plusieurs langues étrangères et effectuent le change aux heures de fermeture des banques, elles donnent des renseignements, etc.

DISTRIBUTEUR AUTOMATIQUE DE DÉPLIANTS
Moyennant 1 F jour et nuit (hôtels, restaurants, plans, heures d'ouverture des châteaux, circuits de jour et de nuit).

TÉLEX
L'Office du Tourisme fait partie de la chaîne « ACCUEIL DE FRANCE » et assure ainsi des réservations hôtelières faites par Télex (n.750008).
D'autre part, cet appareil permet de donner aux touristes des renseignements sur les autres Centres, et ce immédiatement.

VITRINES
L'Office du Tourisme possède de très vastes vitrines. La décoration de celles-ci permet de faire connaître au public les nombreuses manifestations et expositions, ainsi que l'activité touristique, artisanale, culturelle et sportive de la région.

PANNEAU DE DISPONIBILITÉS HOTELIERES
Après la fermeture de l'Office du Tourisme, les hôtels signalés sur le plan lumineux de Tours par des lampes éclairées indiquent les possibilités de chambres libres.

(Ce panneau est situé à l'extérieur de l'Office : une cabine téléphonique est à proximité).

VISITE DE TOURS AUDIO-GUIDÉE
Français - Anglais - Allemand - Espagnol - Italien.

Visite toute l'année
Départ de l'Office du Tourisme.
Renseignements, inscriptions et réservations sur place.

1. Il y a six hôtesses au Syndicat d'Initiative.

2. Elles ne parlent que le français.

3. Au Syndicat d'Initiative on peut changer son argent même quand les banques sont fermées.

4. Si le Syndicat d'Initiative est fermé on peut obtenir des brochures quand même.

5. On peut réserver son hôtel au Syndicat d'Initiative.

7b Look at the services offered by the *Syndicat d'Initiative* again, then answer the questions.

1. What work do the hostesses do?

2. What do you have to do if you want a leaflet and the office is closed?

3. How would you find out information about shows and excursions without even going into the office?

4. When the office is closed, what useful service does the *Syndicat* provide for people who have just arrived in the town and have nowhere to stay?

5. What other useful facility is nearby?

 8a Listen to the cassette. You will hear a conversation between a clerk in the *Syndicat d'Initiative* in Bayonne and a visitor to the town. Say whether these statements are true or false:

1. Le monsieur donne à la dame un plan de la ville.

2. Puis il lui demande une brochure.

3. Malheureusement elle n'a plus de brochures.

4. Le monsieur dit qu'une carte lui serait utile.

5. Il a l'intention de visiter la région.

6. Il demande à la dame s'il y a des excursions intéressantes à faire.

7. Il y a des excursions tous les jours.

8. Il lui demande des dépliants.

9. Les dépliants contiennent tous les détails dont il a besoin.

10. Le monsieur est furieux et impoli.

8b Listen to the conversation again, and write down the expressions which mean:

1. Do you have a town plan?

2. I would like a brochure if you have one.

3. A map of the region;

4. A map would be useful.

5. Are there any interesting excursions?

9 Working with a partner, imagine you are in a *Syndicat d'Initiative*. One of you is a visitor, the other an employee. The visitor wants:

1. a town plan;

2. a brochure about the town;

3. a map of the region;

4. some leaflets about excursions.

The employee offers the town plan and the town brochure, but:

1. says there are no regional maps left;

2. asks what kind of excursions the visitor is interested in;

3. recommends a trip on the river.

Each of you should prepare your role first. When you have acted out the situation, change roles.

10 Listen to the cassette. In the same *Syndicat d'Initiative* a woman is finding out about interesting excursions that week.

1. How often are there trips to Biarritz?

2. What sort of town is Biarritz, according to the man?

3. On what day could the woman go to St Jean de Luz?

4. What is there of interest there?

5. What does the man suggest as a possibility?

6. Why does the woman reject the idea of going to St Sébastien?

7. What is la Rhune?

8. In what country is it situated?

9. How do you get to the top?

10. What details will the woman find on the brochure?

11 Read the details about visiting the cathedral at Boulogne-sur-Mer, then answer the questions.

Boulogne-sur-Mer
La Cathédrale

La Cathédrale : d'autres possibilités.

Des visites plus complètes de ce monument sont organisées de façon régulière l'après-midi à 15 h.

Renseignement au bureau d'accueil de la Cathédrale. Prix de la visite avec crypte par un Guide de Renaissance du Vieux Boulogne :
Adultes : 10 F.
Enfants : 5 F.

2 visites exceptionnelles de la Cathédrale sont organisée les **Mardi 17 Juillet et 21 Août** à 18 heures.

Ces visites-conférences sont faites par un Guide Diplômé

de la Caisse des Monuments Historiques et des Sites et nous feront découvrir tous les aspects de ce monument.

Au programme :
Cathédrale de Boulogne :
son architecture,
son histoire,
les Pèlèrinages,
l'orgue,
la crypte,
le Trésor.

Ces visites sont accompagnées d'oeuvres musicales interprétées par des artistes avec le concours des Amis de l'Orgue de Notre Dame.
Prix Adultes : 20 F.
     Enfants : 10 F.
A ne pas manquer.

1. What is organised at 3 o'clock in the afternoon?

2. How much would it cost two adults and three children to visit the cathedral and its crypt?

3. Where must you go for information about visiting the cathedral?

4. On what dates and at what times are two special visits arranged?

5. Name four aspects of the cathedral that will be described during these visits.

6. What will accompany these visits?

7. What strong recommendation is made about these visits?

12a Imagine you are staying in a French town, and want some information from the *Syndicat d'Initiative*. Your French friend has offered to go there for you, and you jot down (in French) a few notes to help your friend remember what you want to know.

12b You are hoping to visit France shortly, and write to the *Syndicat d'Initiative* of a town you intend to visit. In your letter, you

1. ask for their help;

2. ask what interesting things there are to see and do;

3. ask what trips you might go on;

4. ask them to send you a town plan and some brochures.

13a

Look carefully at the photograph of the castle of Angers and its surroundings, then say whether the statements are true or false.

1. Le château est flanqué d'un grand nombre de tours.

2. Il n'y a pas de pont sur la rivière.

3. Il y a des jardins à l'intérieur du château.

4. Il y a un parking à l'intérieur du château.

5. La circulation passe devant le château.

13b Look again at the photograph of the castle at Angers, then write answers to these questions in French:

1. Comment peut-on traverser la rivière près du château?

2. Où est-ce qu'on peut se promener à l'intérieur du château?

3. Où est-ce qu'on peut garer sa voiture?

4. De quoi le château est-il flanqué?

14 Write a letter to a friend who is shortly coming to spend a holiday with you, telling him/her what there is to visit in your town or a town near where you live.

Un peu de grammaire

The Future

1. Forming the Future Tense

Take the Infinitive of the verb you want to use, e.g. **voyager**. Add to it the ending of the Present Tense of **avoir**, like this:

> voyager: voyager + ai = je voyagerai
> manger: manger + ai = je mangerai
> arriver: arriver + ai = j'arriverai
> partir: partir   + ai = je partirai

If the verb you want to use is an **-re** verb, drop the **e** from the end first, like this:

> descendre: descendr + ai = je descendrai
> attendre: attendr   + ai = j'attendrai
> prendre: prendr   + ai = je prendrai

2. Irregular verbs

A few common verbs are different, and need to be learned separately. These are the main ones:

> être: je serai   devoir: je devrai
> avoir: j'aurai   voir: je verrai
> faire: je ferai   envoyer: j'enverrai
> aller: j'irai   venir: je viendrai
> pouvoir: je pourrai   courir: je courrai

There are no exceptions when it comes to the endings, however. All verbs follow this pattern:

> je voyagerai   nous voyagerons
> tu voyageras   vous voyagerez
> il voyagera   ils voyageront
> elle voyagera   elles voyageront

Voici le troisième épisode de notre feuilleton *Un Voyage en Chemin de Fer*.

Marie-France est en train de demander si la bombe va éclater quand le chef de train revient tout essoufflé en disant que la police et l'armée vont bientôt arriver.

En effet, des sirènes se font déjà entendre, et quelques moments plus tard deux voitures s'arrêtent sur la route qui borde le champ.

Le chef de train, qui semble beaucoup plus courageux que le mécanicien, se précipite vers une des voitures et dit au soldat qui en descend de le suivre.

Marie-France et les autres voyageurs regardent les hommes qui remontent dans le train.

Tout le monde se demande si c'est déjà trop tard ou si le soldat va réussir à empêcher l'explosion.

Un petit garçon se met à pleurer et sa mère essaie de le consoler.

Une vieille femme se fâche et proteste contre les terroristes qui tuent les innocents avec leurs bombes.

Marie-France ne dit rien mais elle regarde sa montre et compte les minutes qui passent: cinq, six, sept... C'est interminable, se dit-elle. Qu'est-ce qui va se passer?

(A SUIVRE)

Unit 11
Vous aimez le sport?

In this unit you will learn to

– discuss your own and other people's sporting activities

– understand discussion on sporting topics

– tell other people what you do in your spare time

– find out what other people do in their spare time

 1a Listen to the cassette. You will hear a conversation between a boy and a girl, who are discussing how they spend their spare time. Now answer the questions.

1. Why doesn't the boy do any sport?

2. When did he last do any?

3. What does he prefer to do instead?

4. Which sports doesn't the girl like?

5. What does she do in winter?

6. What water sports does she do?

7. What else does she do in summer?

8. What did she buy last summer?

 1b Listen to the conversation again, and write down the expression which means:

1. What sport do you do?

2. I don't do any sport.

3. I have never been interested in sport.

4. I like all sports.

5. I play basketball.

6. I go in for water sports.

When you are talking about sport, there are three verbs you are likely to use more than any others, i.e. **pratiquer**, **faire** and **jouer**.

Use **pratiquer**
– if you are talking about sport in general, e.g.

Je pratique tous les sports.

Je pratique les sports d'hiver.

Use **faire**
– wherever you might use **pratiquer**
– for activities which are sports rather than games, e.g.

Je fais du ski.

Tu fais de la planche à voile?

(Notice that here, **faire** is followed by **de**.)

Use **jouer**
– if you are talking about a game rather than a sport, e.g.

Je joue au football.

Tu joues au tennis?
(Notice that **jouer** is followed by **à**; remember that it is followed by **de** when it means to play a musical instrument.)

You can, of course, use other verbs when you are talking about what you *like* doing, e.g.

J'aime le rugby.

Je déteste la boxe.

Je préfère la pêche.

– in other words, you can use the same expressions you learned when talking about food and drink.

1c Listen to the conversation between the boy and girl again, and make a list, in French, of all the sports mentioned.

Other sports which have not yet been mentioned are:

l'aérobic (m)	l'alpinisme (m)	l'athlétisme (m)
le badminton	le cricket	le cross
la danse	l'équitation (f)	la gymnastique
le hockey	le jogging	la natation
le netball	le patinage sur glace	le snooker
le squash	la voile	le volleyball

If you do any sport that is not listed there, ask your teacher what is the French for it.

2 Ask everyone in your class, 'Quels sports fais-tu?', and make a list along these lines:

Trois personnes font du ski.
Quatorze personnes jouent au tennis, etc.
(To keep it within bounds, limit everyone to three sports.)

3 Look at the strip cartoon, then finish each of the statements by adding the most appropriate ending from the choice given.

1. Le chat est
   A au bord de la rivière.
   B dans un jardin public.
   C en montagne.

2. Il veut
   A jouer dans l'eau.
   B laisser tomber la canne à pêche.
   C attraper des poissons.

3. Il finit par
   A tomber par terre.
   B tomber dans l'eau
   C tomber sur sa canne.

142

4   Look at the newspaper cutting giving details of sporting
    activities available in the region, then say whether the
    statements are true or false.

Accueil & loisirs jeunes

BASES DE PLEIN AIR

● **Arras : canoé-kayak**
  Base de loisirs, Mairie, 62223 St-Laurent-Blangy
● **Béthune : voile, canoé-kayak, orientation**
  Base de plein air, Gare d'eau, 62660 Beuvry
● **Courrières : canoé-kayak, orientation**
  Base de plein air, 62710 Courrières
● **Calais : voile, canoé-kayak**
  C.I.S.P.A. base de voile, Fort Risban, 62100 Calais
● **Boulogne : canoé-kayak, cyclo-tourisme, orientation**
  Base nautique canoé, boulevard Chanzy, 62200 Boulogne-sur-Mer
● **Etaples : voile**
  Centre nautique de la Canche, 62630 Etaples-sur-Mer
● **Saint-Omer : canoé-kayak**
  Base de plein air, Fort aux Vaches, 62500 Saint-Omer

Renseignements : D.D.T.L.J.S., 126, rue d'Amiens, 62033
Arras, tél. (21) 23.46.80.

1. A Calais on peut faire de la voile.

2. Si on aime faire du canoé il ne faut pas aller à Arras.

3. Il n'y a qu'un seul centre de cyclisme.

4. On peut pratiquer des sports d'eau à tous ces centres.

5. Il y a plus de centres de voile que d'orientation.

5   Listen to the cassette recording in which you will hear a
    telephone conversation between a boy and a girl, then answer
    the questions.

    1. What does Philippe want Julie to do?

    2. When?

    3. Why doesn't she want to do this?

    4. What does she suggest instead?

    5. Why does Philippe think her suggestion is perhaps better
       than his?

    6. Why is Philippe surprised?

    7. What is Julie afraid of?

    8. What time do they agree to meet?

    9. Where?

6a Listen to the cassette. You will hear another telephone conversation, but this time you will only hear half of it (as you would in real life if you overheard someone talking on the phone). What you hear is printed out, but try and understand it first simply by listening. Then listen again and write down what you think the other person said, so that the conversation is complete

—Allô, qui est à l'appareil?

—......

—Ah, bonjour, Sophie. Oui, ça va bien, merci. Et toi?

—......

—Tu es enrhumée? Oh, mais c'est dommage! Alors, pour cet après-midi, ça va quand même?

—......

—Oui, d'accord, tu as peut-être raison, il vaut mieux ne pas aller se baigner quand on est enrhumé.

—......

—Oui, si tu préfères. Quel film voudrais-tu voir?

—......

– Ah bon. Non, je ne l'ai pas déjà vu, mais j'aime beaucoup les films de James Bond.

—......

—Ça dépend. A quelle heure est-ce que ça commence?

—......

—Bon, alors je te verrai un quart d'heure avant, à trois heures vingt.

—......

—Oh, dans le café qui se trouve en face du cinéma, je crois.

—......

—D'accord, je ne serai pas en retard cette fois! Au revoir!

6b Look at the completed conversation then answer these questions:

1. What is the matter with Sophie?

2. What had Sophie and her friend previously arranged to do?

3. What does she suggest they do instead?

4. What time does it start?

5. Where do they arrange to meet?

6. What does he promise?

7 Write a letter to a French friend saying:

1. what sports you like playing and watching;

2. what sports he/she likes playing and watching;

3. what you are going to do next weekend.

8   Look at the cutting from a magazine which gives details of a television sports programme, then answer the questions.

14.20 SPORTS DIMANCHE

Emission du service des Sports, proposée par Jean-Michel Leulliot.

La 205 GTI, un bolide qui saute les bosses.

AUTOMOBILE : DEFI TF1

En direct de la région de Grenoble. Commentaires : Bernard Giroux.

Quel est le meilleur pilote de rallye ? Difficile de répondre à une telle question en raison des voitures, chacun disposant de véhicules différents. C'est pourquoi cet après-midi une douzaine de pilotes vont s'affronter au volant des mêmes voitures. Une Renault super 5 TSE, une Peugeot 205 GTI et une Citroën BX GT.

Les pilotes en compétition : **Andruet, Darniche, Frequelin, Wambergue, Streiff, Saby, Beltoise, Jabouille, Vatanen.**

HIPPISME : TIERCE

En direct de Vincennes. Commentaires : André Théron.

CROSS DU FIGARO : COURSE DES AS

Course des As. Commentaires : Pierre Toret.
Cette épreuve est en fait, le bouquet final des deux journées qui réunissent généralement 20 000 concurrents. Pour ce cross des As, les principaux favoris sont une nouvelle fois **Boxberger, Levisse, Watrice** et **Bouster.**

CURLING : CHAMPIONNAT D'EUROPE

66   En différé de Morzine. Commentaires : Daniel Pautrat.

1. On what day is this programme being shown?

2. Which programmes are broadcast live?

3. Which is recorded?

4. How many drivers are competing in the car rally?

5. To what question about the car rally is it said to be difficult to give an answer?

6. What are the drivers going to do this afternoon?

7. What is taking place at Vincennes?

8. How long does the Figaro cross-country race last?

9. Who are Boxberger and Levisse?

10. What curling competition is taking place?

9 Read the magazine cutting about the sport of curling, then answer the questions.

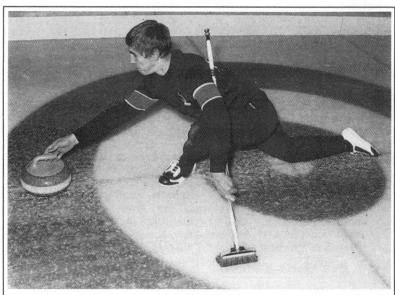

Le curling, un sport venu du froid : il faut savoir pousser la pierre...

EN DIFFÉRÉ DE MORZINE

CURLING

*CHAMPIONNAT
D'EUROPE*

**COMMENTAIRES DE
DANIEL PAUTRAT**

Lorsqu'il est pratiqué au plus haut niveau, le curling est un sport très spectaculaire. Il s'agit, rappelons-le, de faire glisser une pierre (d'un poids légèrement inférieur à 20 kg) sur une piste de glace vers une cible tracée sur le sol. Pour accélérer ou freiner la pierre, les joueurs peuvent balayer la glace. A ce jeu, les meilleurs sont les Écossais et les Suédois.

1. From what sort of countries does this game come?

2. What do the players have to do with the curling stones?

3. According to this article, what kind of sport is curling when it is played at the highest level?

4. What is the weight of the stone?

5. What sort of surface is the game played on?

6. Where does the stone have to finish up?

7. Why do players sweep the ice?

8. From what countries do the best players come?

10a Read this advertisement and then answer the questions.

Vous faites partie d'une équipe de basket, d'un club de tennis, ou vous courez tous les marathons de France et de Navarre? La chaîne d'hôtels Ibis se propose de vous loger à des prix Spécial Sportifs lorsque vous vous déplacez pour une compétition. 99 F la chambre pour une, deux ou trois personnes. Vraiment pas cher pour un hôtel de catégorie deux étoiles! Pour réserver, contactez l'hôtel de votre choix et précisez la nature de la compétition qui motive votre petit voyage. Confirmez ensuite le nombre de participants par courrier, et vous recevrez une réponse écrite de l'hôtel. Rien de plus simple!

1. What sort of people is this advertisement aimed at?

2. When could they take up this offer?

3. What sort of rooms are available?

4. At what price?

5. What sort of hotels are they?

6. What do you have to do to make a booking?

10b Imagine you would like to take up the offer, and write to a hotel to make a booking. Make sure you say when you want to go, for how long, why, how many people will be in your party, and how many rooms you want.

11a Listen to the cassette. You will hear an extract from a radio broadcast. Say whether these statements are true or false:

1. This is the ninth international athletics meeting to be held in Nice.

2. It was held the night before this broadcast.

3. Joaquim Cruz holds the world record for 1000 metres.

4. France gained two pole-vaulting medals at the last Olympic Games.

5. Joseph Mahmoud is running in the 3000 metres steeplechase.

6. Mahmoud won a silver medal in the Olympic Games.

11b Listen to the broadcast again, then answer these questions:

1. When is the meeting to be held?

2. At what distance is Joaquim Cruz running?

3. What does he hope to do?

4. What is the nationality of the two pole-vaulters mentioned?

5. What event is Mahmoud running in?

6. What mistake does the interviewer make?

7. Why does Mahmoud say he is going into unknown territory?

147

12 Look at the cartoon, then imagine that you are telling a French friend about it. What would you say? Remember to tell your friend:

1. who is involved;
2. what they have been doing;
3. what has happened to them;
4. where they are now;
5. what one says to the other.

—Veinarde! On m'a assuré que le mien était blanc, mais votre plâtre est encore plus blanc!

13a Read this extract from a French newspaper dealing with another athletics meeting, then answer the questions.

Athlétisme à Cologne

Un des 800 m les plus rapides de l'histoire

Le Britannique, Sebastian Coe a presque perdu son record du monde (1'41"73) à la réunion d'athlétisme de Cologne quand le Brésilien, Joaquim Cruz, champion olympique du 800 m, a réalisé 1'41"77, c'est-à-dire à peine quatre centièmes de seconde de plus que Coe.

C'est Thomas Giessing de l'Allemagne de l'Ouest qui a servi de lièvre à Cruz en passant aux 400 m en 49"53. C'est seulement à 200 m de l'arrivée que Cruz s'est détaché et a réussi une extraordinaire fin de course, établissant le deuxième meilleur «chrono» de tous les temps, aussi bien qu'une nouvelle meilleure performance mondiale de l'année. Le Kenyan, Sammy Koskei, qui est arrivé deuxième derrière Cruz a établi la troisième meilleure performance de tous les temps (1'42"28).

Pierre Quinon, le champion olympique de la perche, s'est aussi mis en évidence en battant encore une fois les Américains. Il a sauté 5,70 m tandis que les Américains Earl Bell et Doug Lytle ont sauté 5,60 m et le deuxième Français, Thierry Vigneron, a sauté 5,50 m.

1. By how much did Cruz miss beating Coe's record?

2. Over what distance was he running?

3. At what point did Cruz take the lead?

4. Who acted as pace-maker?

5. What country does the pace-maker come from?

6. Who came second?

7. Who won the pole-vault?

 13b Imagine that you were at one of these meetings. You write a letter to a French friend telling him or her about what happened in one of the events. Remember that in a letter to a friend you would not write in the same way as a reporter writes in a newspaper. Say where the meeting was, when, who you went with, what event you found most exciting, who won it and in what time, whether a record was beaten, and give any other information you think might be interesting.

13c Here are the results of two of the events at the Nikaïa:

1 000 mètres hommes
Record du monde: COE Sebastian (Grande Bretagne) 2'12"18 (1981)
1. CRUZ Joaquim (Brésil) 2'14"09 (*record du stade*)
2. WILLIAMSON Graham (Grande Bretagne) 2'16"86
3. McGEORGE Chris (Grande Bretagne) 2'17"45

5 000 mètres hommes
Record du monde: MOORCROFT Dave (Grande Bretagne) 13'00"41 (1982)
1. BACCOUCHE Fethi (Tunisie) 13'46"53
2. DIEMER Brian (Etats-Unis) 13'47"37
3. MAHMOUD Joseph (France) 13'48"19

Imagine that, while on a camping holiday in France, you went to the athletics meeting at Nice. On returning to the campsite you talk to a French boy or girl about the meeting. He/she asks you these questions. What would you say?

1. Qui a gagné les mille mètres?

2. C'est un Français?

3. C'était un nouveau record du monde?

4. Qui a le record du monde?

5. Il vient de quel pays, lui?

6. Qui est arrivé deuxième et troisième?

7. Mahmoud a couru?

8. Sur quelle distance?

9. Il a gagné?

10. Qu'est-ce qu'il a donc fait?

13d Working with a partner, work out a conversation you might have had with that French boy or girl. Decide who is to play which part, then act out the situation. Make sure that your conversation deals with these points:

1. where and when the meeting was held;

2. who you went with;

3. which events were the most exciting;

4. what happened in the 800 metres and the 1000 metres;

5. why you, coming from Great Britain, had reason to feel pleased.

Un peu de grammaire

If you want to talk about something that is going to happen in the future, you do not have to use the Future Tense, especially if it is going to happen fairly soon; you simply use the present Tense of the verb **aller**, followed by another verb, like this:

Je vais aller en Espagne.

Il va visiter Bordeaux.

Nous allons prendre le train.

Ils vont passer un mois en Bretagne.

This construction is used a great deal in conversation, much more often than the Future Tense, which is a little more formal.

You can also use it like this, with the Imperfect of the verb **aller**, still followed by an infinitive:

Il allait prendre le train quand un homme lui a crié.

– which tells you what someone *was* going to do before something happened to stop it.

NOTRE FEUILLETON

Voici le quatrième épisode de notre feuilleton *Un Voyage en Chemin de Fer*.

Huit, neuf, dix minutes et rien n'arrive. Mais si, le soldat et le mécanicien apparaissent enfin.

—N'ayez plus peur, dit le soldat. Il n'y aura pas d'explosion. J'ai pu désamorcer la bombe et vous pouvez tous reprendre vos places dans le train.

Le mécanicien ajoute qu'on a cherché partout et qu'on n'a pas trouvé d'autres paquets cachés dans le train.

Un peu plus tard le train se remet en marche, mais Marie-France se pose toujours des questions.

Pourquoi a-t-on mis cette bombe dans le train? Quel voyageur veut-on tuer?

Y a-t-il quelqu'un de très important parmi les voyageurs—un homme politique, peut-être? Est-ce le vieux monsieur, ou le jeune homme, qui sont assis tout près d'elle?

Ne pouvant répondre à ces questions Marie-France cesse d'y penser et reprend son illustré.

Elle ne trouve pas l'article sur la première page très intéressant et se sentant fatiguée elle ferme les yeux et elle est sur le point de s'endormir quand...

... le train ralentit et puis s'arrête encore une fois.

—Ce n'est pas possible, pense Marie-France. Y a-t-il une seconde bombe dans le train?

(A SUIVRE)

Unit 12
A la poste

In this unit you will learn about

– postal services in France

– asking about postage costs

– buying stamps

– using the telephone

– taking phone messages

1a Read this information about French postal services, then answer the questions which follow.

Aux PTT vous pouvez
—acheter des timbres
—envoyer des paquets
—envoyer un télégramme
—envoyer ou recevoir de l'argent par des mandats
—téléphoner à quelqu'un

Si vous voulez acheter des timbres-poste il faut aller dans un bureau de tabac ou à la poste.

Si vous voulez poster une lettre il faut chercher une boîte aux lettres que vous trouverez aux PTT, près des bureaux de tabac ou dans la rue.

Pour tous ces services et pour les autres services postaux il faut chercher les PTT—c'est-à-dire les Poste-Téléphone-Télécommunications. Dans une grande ville il y a toujours une grande poste et aussi des bureaux de poste. Chaque bureau de poste porte cette enseigne.

1. What can you do at the post office?

2. Where else could you go to buy stamps?

3. In what places would you find a letter box?

4. How would you recognise a post office?

1b Read the information again, then write down the expressions which mean:

1. the post office;
2. a letter box;
3. a postage stamp;
4. a tobacconist's;
5. a sign;
6. a parcel;
7. a postal order;
8. a telegram.

2 Read this information, then say whether the statements are true or false.

> **... expédier vos envois**
>
> ● **Les timbres-poste :** vous pouvez vous les procurer dans les bureaux de poste (où on vend également des aérogrammes), les bureaux de tabac ou les distributeurs automatiques jaunes disposés sur la façade de certains bureaux de poste (ils fonctionnent avec de la monnaie).

> ● **Les boîtes de dépôt des lettres :** vous les trouverez à l'extérieur et à l'intérieur des bureaux de poste mais aussi près des bureaux de tabac et lieux de fort passage du public .

1. Pour acheter des timbres il faut aller à la poste.
2. On peut acheter des timbres dans un bureau de tabac.
3. Les distributeurs de timbres sont rouges.
4. Vous ne trouverez pas de boîtes aux lettres dans la rue.
5. Vous trouverez des boîtes aux lettres à l'intérieur du bureau de poste.

3 Read this information about posting parcels, then answer the questions.

> ● **Paquets :** les paquets adressés à d'autres pays jusqu'à 1 kg (ou 2 kg au tarif des lettres) acceptés par les bureaux de poste doivent porter extérieurement une étiquette verte de douane. Si vous voulez réaliser un envoi rationnel et pratique, utilisez les emballages préformés mis en vente dans les bureaux de poste.
> ● **Colis postaux :** les colis postaux sont acceptés au bureau de poste principal de chaque localité.
> – "Avion" jusqu'à 10 ou 20 kg suivant la destination.
> – "Voie de surface" jusqu'à 5 kg et jusqu'à un certain format pour tous pays (au-delà de ces limites de poids ou de dimension, les colis postaux "voie de surface" peuvent être confiés à la SNCF).

1. What colour is the customs label on a parcel going abroad?
2. Why do post offices sell special packaging for parcels?
3. How will large parcels weighing 10 to 20 kilos travel?
4. What is the top weight for surface mail accepted by post offices?
5. How does heavier surface mail travel?
6. Is this service available just within France?

To buy stamps, you need to say which stamps you require. A stamp that costs 2 francs is

un timbre à deux francs

A stamp that costs 4 francs 20 is

un timbre à quatre francs vingt

So if you want three stamps at 2 francs 40, you say:

Trois timbres à deux francs quarante, s'il vous plaît.

If you don't know what the postage is, you ask:

Combien coûte une lettre pour l'Angleterre, s'il vous plaît?
or
Une lettre pour l'Angleterre, ça coûte combien?

4a Listen to the cassette recording in which you will hear a man buying stamps, then answer the questions.

1. What does the man want to send?

2. How many stamps does he buy at (i) 2 F 40? (ii) 1 F 70?

3. How much does he have to pay?

4b Listen to the cassette recording in which you will hear a lady buying stamps, then answer the questions.

1. How many stamps does she buy at 2 F 10?

2. Where does she want to send a letter by air mail?

3. How much will this cost?

4. How much does she have to pay altogether?

4c Listen to the two conversations again, then write down the expressions which mean:

1. How much is a stamp for England?

2. I have two letters and four postcards.

3. How much does that come to altogether?

4. I would like some stamps, please.

5. three stamps at 2 F 10;

6. an airmail letter.

4d Working with a partner, imagine you are in a post office or a tobacconist's shop. Decide which of you will be the customer and which the assistant, then act out the situation.

The customer will:

1. ask how much it costs to send a letter;

2. buy six stamps at the price given;

3. ask where the letter box is.

The assistant will say:

1. how much it costs to send a letter;

2. how much the customer owes for the six stamps;

3. where the letter box is.

After acting out the situation, change roles, using different prices and a different place for the letter box.

 5 If the post office or tobacconist's are shut, you may find an 'automatic post office' like the one in the photograph, which actually weighs your letter or packet and then tells you how much it will cost. Read these instructions, then answer the questions.

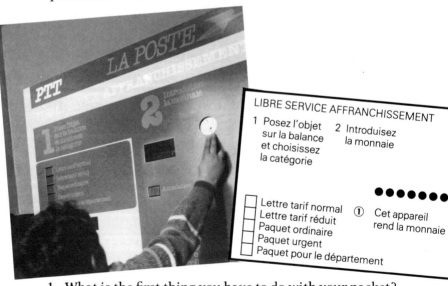

1. What is the first thing you have to do with your packet?

2. What must you do next?

3. What do you do to get your stamps?

4. What happens if you don't have the right money?

6 Read this newspaper item about a very special stamp, then
   answer the questions.

Un timbre qui coûte 9 millions de francs

Un acheteur anonyme—collectionneur de timbres-poste—a payé 2,3 millions de
marks, c'est-à-dire 9 millions de francs, à Wiesbaden samedi dernier pour acquérir le
timbre le plus cher du monde. Ce timbre qui date de 1851 fait partie de «l'impression
manquée de Bade» et a été vendu aux enchères. Son ancien propriétaire était un
multi-millionnaire américain, John Boker.

  Quand ce timbre de neuf kreutzer a été émis il y a cent trente-quatre ans en Pays de
Bade, il a été imprimé par erreur sur du papier vert, couleur du timbre de six kreutzer.
On n'a découvert l'erreur qu'en 1884 et il existe seulement deux autres exemplaires
de cette «impression manquée».

1. What is special about this stamp?

2. How was it sold?

3. Who bought it?

4. Who did it belong to before that?

5. How long ago was it issued?

6. What printing error was made?

7. How many years passed before the error was discovered?

8. How many other stamps are there like this one?

 7a Listen to the cassette recording in which you will hear a
   conversation between a post-office clerk and a lady who wants
   to send a parcel, then answer the questions.

1. How much does the parcel weigh?

2. How much does it cost?

3. What does the lady have to write on the label?

4. What must she do with the label then?

 7b Listen to the conversation again, then write down the
   expressions which mean:

1. I would like to send this parcel.

2. I'll weigh it.

3. It weighs...

4. the person it is addressed to,

5. to stick.

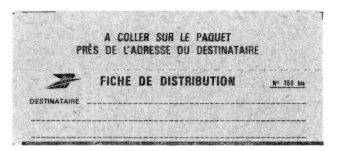

A COLLER SUR LE PAQUET
PRÈS DE L'ADRESSE DU DESTINATAIRE

FICHE DE DISTRIBUTION   N° 759 bis

DESTINATAIRE

7c This label is like the one the lady had to stick on her parcel. Where exactly must it be stuck?

7d Practise the parcel dialogue with a friend, then invent similar ones of your own.

8a Read the information about the telephone service, then say whether the statements are true or false.

Si vous voulez téléphoner il faut chercher une cabine téléphonique que vous trouverez également dans la rue, aux PTT, à la gare, dans les cafés, etc.

Voici un plan de ville qui montre les PTT et les cabines téléphoniques ou les groupes de cabines téléphoniques dans un quartier près du port de Mandelieu-La Napoule, près de Cannes, dans le Midi de la France.

● indique qu'il y a une cabine à cet endroit,
★ indique qu'il y en a deux,
○ indique qu'il y en a au moins trois.

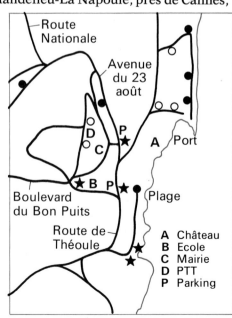

Route Nationale

Avenue du 23 août

Port

Plage

Boulevard du Bon Puits

Route de Théoule

A Château
B Ecole
C Mairie
D PTT
P Parking

1. Le bureau de poste est près de la mairie.

2. Il y a trois cabines téléphoniques tout près de la poste.

3. Il y a très peu de cabines téléphoniques près du port.

4. Si vous voulez téléphoner quand vous êtes sur la plage, vous n'avez pas besoin de quitter la plage.

5. Il y a deux cabines près de l'école.

6. Il n'y a pas de cabines téléphoniques près des parkings.

8b Work with a partner. One of you looks at the map, and answers questions asked by the other. The person asking questions says, 'Je suis au château. Où est la cabine téléphonique la plus proche, s'il vous plaît?', and then asks how to get there. Check that you have understood the directions, then change roles. (Other locations you might use are: à la plage, dans le Boulevard du Bon Puits, sur la Route de Théoule, dans l'Avenue du 23 août.)

Here are some useful expressions about telephoning:

un annuaire des téléphones	*telephone directory*
décrocher l'appareil	*to lift the receiver*
raccrocher l'appareil	*to replace the receiver*
composer le numéro	*to dial the number*
un indicatif	*dialling code*
la tonalité	*dialling tone*
le tarif	*rate*
un abonné	*subscriber*
une communication	*call*
urbain	*within a town*
interurbain	*between two towns*
en dérangement	*out of order*
occupé	*engaged*
en PCV	*reverse charge*
se tromper de numéro	*to get the wrong number*
Allô	*Hallo (only used on the telephone)*
Qui est à l'appareil?	*Who is speaking?*
C'est de la part de qui?	*Who is speaking?*
Ne quittez pas	*Hold the line*
rappeler	*to call back*
couper la communication	*to cut off the call*

9 These are various signs and notices you would see in a telephone box. Look at them carefully and then answer the questions.

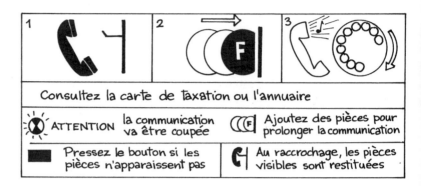

Aidez-nous à assurer un meilleur service en signalant toute anomalie de fonctionnement.
Appelez gratuitement le 13.
Précisez le numéro figurant sur la cabine.

1. What is the number of this telephone box?

2. What can you consult if you want to find a number?

3. Which instruction tells you you are about to be cut off?

4. What can you do to gain more time?

5. When may you need to press the button?

6. What happens when you replace the receiver?

7. How can the user obtain a better service?

8. What detail must you give if you dial 13?

10 Look at the extract from a telephone users' guide, and then answer the questions.

TELEPHONEZ EN COULEUR !

● VOUS EVITEZ LES HEURES D'ENCOMBREMENT
● VOUS TELEPHONEZ A PRIX REDUIT

REDUCTION DE :

65%	50%	30%	Tarif Normal
TARIF GRIS NUIT	TARIF GRIS	TARIF BLANC	TARIF ROUGE

TABLEAU DES COMMUNICATIONS INTERURBAINES*

	23h.	6h.	8h.	14h.	18h.	21h.30	23h.
LUNDI au VENDREDI							
SAMEDI							
DIMANCHE & FETES							

Tarif réduit pour le Canada, Etats-Unis, Israël, Belgique R.F.A. Danemark, Grèce, Irlande du Sud, Italie, Luxembourg Pays-Bas, Royaume-Uni: Voir conditions dans l'annuaire.
*Tarif au 15 Mai 1986

VOUS SOUHAITEZ

● **Demander un renseignement** .... **appelez le 12**
(mais pensez d'abord à l'annuaire)

● **Signaler un dérangement** .... **appelez le 13**

● **Envoyer un télégramme** .... **appelez le 00.11.11**

● **Demander une communication spéciale**
(A.V.P., P.C.V., etc.) .... **appelez le 10**

● **Pour l'étranger composez le 19 . . . 33 . . . et l'indicatif du pays.**

● **Demander un abonnement:**
voir Agence commerciale ou Téléboutique (plan), ou ...... **appelez le 14**

1. At what times of day is it cheapest to use the telephone?

2. At what times of day is it most expensive to use the telephone?

3. Which is the cheapest day of the week to telephone?

4. Where can you find details of the reduced rates for telephoning foreign countries?

5. Why would you dial these numbers?
   (i) 12, (ii) 00.11.11, (iii) 10.

11 Listen to the cassette. You will hear a woman taking a phone message for her son, who is out. Now answer the questions.

1. Where has Marc gone?

2. What time should the match have been?

3. What time will it be now?

4. Where will the boys meet?

12 Listen to the cassette. You will hear another conversation in which a message is taken. Write the message down in French. (There is no need to take it down word for word, but the important items must be there.)

13 Listen to the cassette. You will hear a number of telephone messages. Imagine that you are staying with a French family, and are alone in the house. The telephone rings, and you are asked to take a message. In each case write down the message in French. (There is no need to take it down word for word, but the important items must be there.)

14 Les PTT n'emploient plus les pigeons pour livrer le courrier, mais ces oiseaux servent toujours à quelque chose. Lisez cet extrait d'un journal, puis répondez aux questions.

Pigeons sauveteurs

Tout le monde sait que les pigeons servaient autrefois à porter des messages, mais savez-vous qu'ils aident maintenant à sauver les victimes des naufrages? Ce sont les Américains qui entraînent des équipes de pigeons sauveteurs.

On apprend aux oiseaux à appuyer du bec sur un écran de contrôle chaque fois qu'ils voient un objet rouge, jaune ou orange—ces trois couleurs sont les couleurs traditionnelles des combinaisons et signaux de sauvetage. Puis on installe les pigeons dans une cage transparente à bord d'un hélicoptère qui vole au-dessus de la mer. Ces oiseaux remarquables repèrent des cibles à une distance de plus de cinq cents mètres.

1. What kind of people are the pigeons now helping?

2. Who is training the pigeons?

3. In what kind of vehicle do the pigeons travel?

4. Where are the pigeons placed?

5. How do the pigeons press the control screen?

6. When do they do this?

7. From how far off can pigeons see targets?

Un peu de grammaire

Negatives

Negatives are expressions like:

ne ... pas	*not*
ne ... plus	*no more, no longer*
ne ... personne	*nobody*
ne ... rien	*nothing*
ne ... jamais	*never*
ne ... aucun	*not any*
ne ... que	*only*

In a simple tense like the Present, Future or Imperfect, you just place the **ne** before the verb and the second part of the negative after the verb, e.g.

Je ne joue pas au football.

Il n'ira jamais en Russie.

Elle ne mange plus de bonbons.

In a compound tense like the Perfect or the Pluperfect, you place the **ne** before the auxiliary verb (**avoir** or **être**), and the second part of the negative after the auxiliary but before the past participle, e.g.

Je n'ai jamais été sportif.

Tu n'as rien fait hier.

Elle n'a aucune idée.

Personne is an exception to this, as it must be placed after the past participle, e.g.

Il n'a vu personne.

The **que** of **ne ... que** must be placed before the noun to which it refers, e.g.

Je ne suis allé en France qu'une fois.

Elle n'a mangé que deux bonbons.

Remember too that the second part of some of these negatives can stand on its own without **ne** when it is used in answer to a question, e.g.

Qu'est-ce que tu fais? – Rien.

Es-tu allé en France? – Jamais.

Qui as-tu vu? – Personne.

NOTRE FEUILLETON

Voici le dernier épisode de notre feuilleton *Un Voyage en Chemin de Fer*.

Marie-France se lève et sort dans le couloir. D'autres voyageurs en font de même, voulant savoir ce qui se passe.

Cette fois on n'a pas entendu la sonnette d'alarme, et personne ne crie «Descendez du train!». Deux ou trois passagers qui ont peur ouvrent tout de même les portières et vont descendre sur la voie quand le chef de train passe dans le couloir en disant:
—Ne vous inquiétez pas.

—Il n'y a pas de bombe, reprend-il. Il y a une vache sur la voie.

Marie-France éclate de rire et rentre dans son compartiment. La pauvre vache, pense-t-elle, c'est elle qui doit avoir peur maintenant!

Peu après le train roule encore vers Marseille et Marie-France pense à ses parents qui l'attendent sur le quai.
—Ils ne vont pas me croire quand j'explique pourquoi le train a deux heures de retard, pense-t-elle. C'est incroyable, toutes ces aventures de bombes et de vaches!

Comme Marie-France sourit en pensant à cela, un bruit se fait entendre. C'est encore les freins du train qui grincent et Marie-France sursaute.

Mais cette fois le grincement de freins annonce simplement que le train est enfin arrivé à sa destination.

Marie-France et les autres passagers peuvent donc descendre enfin, heureux d'en être quittes pour la peur!

(FIN)

In this unit you will learn

– how to talk about work you do or would like to do

– how to talk about work that others do

– how to apply for a job

1   Read this short extract from a magazine article.

Malgré les problèmes du chômage, la plupart des jeunes Français veulent bien travailler pour gagner leur vie. Ils cherchent un poste intéressant et bien payé et pour ceci ils sont prêts à étudier ou à faire un apprentissage pour apprendre leur métier.

Write down the French for

1. unemployment;   6. well paid;

2. to work;   7. to study;

3. to earn their living;   8. an apprenticeship;

4. to look for;   9. to learn;

5. an interesting job;   10. a trade.

2   Now look at the illustrations which accompanied that article, then write down the French for:

1. a photographer   2. a veterinary secretary
3. a commercial translator   4. a dietitian
5. an accountant   6. a flower arranger
7. a beautician   8. a handwriting expert
9. a social worker   10. a physiotherapist
11. a private secretary   12. a window dresser
13. a computer operator   14. a fashion designer
15. a nursery assistant   16. a dog groomer

AUXILIAIRE DE PUERICULTURE · DIETETICIENNE · SECRETAIRE DE DIRECTION · COMMERCE INTERNATIONAL · REPORTER PHOTOGRAPHE

PROGRAMMEUR D'APPLICATION · ASSISTANTE SOCIALE · MASSEUR KINESITHERAPEUTE · COMPTABLE · PUBLICITE

DESSINATRICE DE MODE · SECRETAIRE ASSISTANTE VETERINAIRE · SECRETAIRE MEDICO-SOCIALE · GRAPHOLOGUE · COMPTABLE SUR INFORMATIQUE

TRADUCTRICE COMMERCIALE · DECORATRICE · ANALYSTE PROGRAMMEUR · EDUCATRICE DE JEUNES ENFANTS · ESTHETICIENNE

CAPACITE EN DROIT · COMMIS DE MAIRIE · ETALAGISTE · TOILETTEUSE DE CHIENS · AUXILIAIRE DE JARDINS D'ENFANT

HOTESSE DU TOURISME · BIBLIOTHECAIRE DOCUMENTALISTE · EDUCATRICE SPORTIVE · OPERATRICE SUR ORDINATEUR · DECORATRICE FLORALE

3a Listen to the cassette recording in which you will hear two boys discussing what they would like to do when they leave school, then answer the questions.

1. What does the first boy want to study at university?

2. If he is unable to find a job with computers, what might he become?

3. What job will the second boy look for once he has completed his military service?

4. What does the girl who can't sit in an office all day want to do?

5. What does her brother say about hospital patients?

3b Listen to the conversation again, then write down the French for:

1. Have you decided what you are going to do for a living?

2. I'd like to go to university.

3. I'll perhaps be an engineer.

4. Have you any ideas?

5. I'll look for a job in an office.

6. What sort of work is she going to do?

7. She doesn't want to sit in an office all day.

Here are some useful phrases to help you talk about what work you would like to do:

Qu'est-ce que tu vas faire dans la vie?

Je voudrais ⎫ être...
            ⎬ devenir...
J'aimerais ⎭ travailler comme...

Je ne sais pas encore

Je ne suis pas sûr(e).

Je chercherai un emploi

un travail

un poste

une situation

intéressant	des vacances payées
passionnant	les heures de travail
un bon salaire	le patron
gagner de l'argent	un collègue
bien payé	

4 Working with a partner, look at all the expressions given above, and take it in turns to ask each other:

Qu'est-ce que tu vas faire dans la vie?

Quelle sorte de poste cherches-tu?

Give a different answer each time.

168

5a Listen to the cassette. You will hear a girl talking to her father about what she wants to do. Say whether these statements are true or false:

1. The girl doesn't like being at school.

2. She wants to be a hotel receptionist.

3. She did well in English at school.

4. She wants to carry on with her languages.

5. She likes the idea of meeting people.

6. Her father thinks she should work on a newspaper.

7. Her father thinks he might have seen something useful for her.

5b Listen to the conversation again, and then answer the questions.

1. What does the girl want to do?

2. Why is her father worried about her ability to do this?

3. What two ways does she suggest of improving her qualifications?

4. Why does she want to do this job?

5. What has her father seen in a newspaper?

6a Look at the advertisement from a newspaper, then say whether the statements are true or false.

1. To use this service you need to have access to a computer.

2. You can use this service to apply for a job.

3. If you are interested in a job in journalism, this service will give you information about vacancies.

4. It is only for school-leavers.

169

6b Look at the advertisement again, then write down the expressions which mean:

1. recruiting;
4. businesses;

2. employment;
5. to dial.

3. the press;

7 Imagine that you would like to work in France. You are going to telephone a French friend who will help you find a job, but before you do so you work out what you are going to say. Working with a partner, decide what you need to tell your friend and how you would say it.

8a Look at the advertisement, and then answer the questions.

1. What kind of jobs are being offered?

2. What two conditions must male applicants satisfy?

3. In what two ways can they contact the company?

4. What one condition must female applicants satisfy?

5. What do they have to do to apply, and when?

8b Listen to the cassette. You will hear a conversation between a young man and M. Bautes of Gestetner. The young man has seen the advertisement above and is telephoning to arrange an interview. Answer the questions.

1. What is the young man's name?

2. After giving his name, what is the first thing he tells M. Bautes?

3. What is the first thing M. Bautes wants to know?

4. What is the young man's answer?

5. What does M. Bautes want to know about his experience?

6. What experience has he had?

7. When is he available to start work?

8. When is his appointment for?

9a Read this letter, written by a young man in response to a newspaper advertisement. Answer the questions on page 172.

Paris, le 17 juin

John Sinclair,
8 rue des Grenelles,
Paris.

Monsieur Georges Legrand,
Les Galeries Junot,
Paris.

Monsieur,

En réponse à l'annonce parue dans 'Le Figaro' du 15 juin, je me permets de poser ma candidature au poste de vendeur que vous proposez pour le mois d'août.

J'ai seize ans et je suis étudiant. Je serai donc libre de travailler pendant les vacances scolaires. Je suis Anglais mais j'habite Paris avec ma famille depuis un an et je parle couramment le français. Nous partirons en vacances en juillet mais nous resterons à Paris en août. Je pourrai donc commencer à travailler quand vous voudrez.

Si vous voulez me voir je me présenterai chez vous à une date qui vous convient.

Veuillez agréer, Monsieur, l'expression de mes sentiments les plus distingués.

John Sinclair

1. Where did John see the job advertised?

2. When?

3. What kind of job is it?

4. During what period does the employer want someone to work?

5. How old is John?

6. What does he do normally?

7. How long has he been living in Paris?

8. What does he say about his ability to speak French?

9. When does he go on holiday?

10. When can he start work?

11. When can he go for an interview?

9b Read this letter, which is a reply to the one on page 171. Unfortunately John spilt coffee on it, and some of the words, or parts of words, were deleted. Write out the letter in full, inserting the missing words. (The letter written by John will help you.)

Monsieur G⬛⬛⬛ Legrand,   Paris le 20 juin
Les Galeries Junot,
Paris.

                                    ⬛⬛eur John Sinclair,
                                    8 rue des Grenelles,
                                    Paris.

Monsieur,

J'ai bien ⬛⬛ votre lettre du ⬛ juin au
sujet de mon annonce dans le Fi⬛⬛⬛

Je pense ⬛⬛ vous pourrez très bien rem⬛⬛ le
poste de vendeur dans ce maga⬛⬛ au mois d'⬛⬛
Etant Anglais, vous parlerez facilem⬛⬛ avec tou⬛
les touristes anglais et américain⬛ qu⬛ passeront
leurs vacances à Paris.

Voulez-vous ven⬛ me vo⬛⬛⬛credi le 22 juin à
trois he⬛⬛ de l'après-midi? J'attendrai cette date
pour vous donn⬛ les conditions de travail dans
ce magasin.

En attend⬛⬛ le plaisir de vous voir, je vous
pr⬛ de croire, Monsieur, à l'assurance de mes
meilleurs sentime⬛⬛

                              Georges Legrand.
                                    Gérant.

172

9c Look at the completed letter, and then answer these questions:

1. What does M. Legrand think is John's biggest asset?

2. What sort of customers is John likely to deal with?

3. On what day does M. Legrand want John to go and see him?

4. At what time?

5. What will he tell him then?

10 Look at this advertisement, which has been placed by someone who is actually looking for a job, then answer the questions.

1. When does the man want to start work?

2. What sort of work is he looking for?

3. Which languages does he speak fluently?

4. What other language does he know?

Personnel hôtelier

Paris, homme recherche à partir du 1-10-82 dans hôtellerie comme réceptionniste. Parle couramment anglais. Allemand, connaissances français. Ecrire sous n° 21132 à SOPIC, B.P. 67001 STRASBOURG.

11 Imagine you want to get a job in France during the holidays, and you have asked a French friend to place an advertisement in the newspaper for you. Your friend has asked you what details you want in the advertisement. Make some notes in French for your friend, giving your age, saying when you want to start, how long you want to work for, what sort of job you want, and giving any other details you think might be useful.

12 Imagine you are being interviewed for a job. Give answers.

1. Quel âge avez-vous?

2. Où habitez-vous?

3. Vous êtes de quelle nationalité?

4. Quelles langues parlez-vous?

5. Quelle expérience avez-vous?

6. Quand est-ce que vous pouvez commencer le travail?

7. Quelles matières avez-vous étudiées à l'école?

13 Imagine that a friend's parents have asked you to write a letter in French for them. They want a French girl to come and look after their two children, aged 4 and 2, for a year starting at the beginning of September. They want someone who likes children, who speaks English, and who is not older than 24. Write a letter on their behalf to an agency in Paris.

14 Listen to the cassette. You will hear a young man talking about what he wanted to do when he was at school and what he finally did. Say whether these statements are true or false:

1. He joined his school orchestra at the age of sixteen.

2. He played an instrument in the orchestra.

3. He threw his microphone into the air.

4. The music they played was rather boring.

5. They played to large audiences.

6. When he left school he planned to form his own band.

7. He ended up working in an office.

15a Listen to the cassette recording in which you will hear a telephone conversation between two girls, then answer the questions.

1. What is the name of the girl making the phone call?

2. Who does she want to speak to?

3. Who answers the phone?

4. Why can't she speak to the person she wanted?

5. Why is she tired?

6. What sort of job has she got?

7. Who does she have to telephone in her job?

8. In what languages does she have to write letters?

9. Why doesn't the other girl think she could cope with that job?

10. What does the caller ask the other girl to do?

11. What does the other girl write down?

12. What is her telephone number?

 15b Working with a partner, listen to the conversation between the two girls again, and work out together a similar conversation using different names and a different job.

Un peu de grammaire

Often in a phrase or sentence one verb is closely linked to another. We say, for example, that we 'can sing', we 'want to sleep', we 'like going' to France, etc.

In French the second of the two verbs will nearly always be in the infinitive, e.g. **chanter**, **venir**, **faire**.

In some cases it will come directly after the first verb, as with:

pouvoir — vous pouvez téléphoner au café

devoir — il doit acheter un timbre

vouloir — je veux envoyer un télégramme

aller — elle va parler à son amie

venir — ils viennent souvent me voir

But in other cases you need to use the word **à** first, as with:

inviter — je t'invite à venir chez moi

commencer — nous commençons à avoir faim

aider — ma mère m'aide à faire mes devoirs

apprendre — ils apprennent à conduire

Some verbs use **de** instead, as with:

décider — j'ai décidé de faire une promenade

avoir besoin — il a besoin d'aller aux magasins

refuser — elle a refusé de m'accompagner

cesser — il a cessé de pleuvoir

In this unit you will learn

– how to talk about events that you have witnessed or heard about

– how to understand news items in newspapers and on the radio

1a Listen to the cassette. You will hear a boy talking to his mother. When you have heard their conversation, complete the sentences by choosing the most suitable option.

1. When Antoine returned, his family
   A hadn't had lunch.
   B were eating their lunch late.
   C had just finished lunch.
   D had finished lunch an hour earlier.

2. The old man was walking
   A on the same side of the street as Antoine.
   B on the other side of the street.
   C in front of the delicatessen.
   D just behind a young man.

3. The thief
   A ran across the road.
   B took the old man's stick.
   C escaped into a narrow passage.
   D disappeared in the traffic.

4. Antoine went to the police station
   A after taking the old man home.
   B straight after the robbery.
   C when he had caught the thief.
   D when he had told someone what he had seen.

5. The policeman wanted to know.
   A where the old man lived.
   B whether the old man wanted to make an official complaint.
   C whether the old man was willing to talk about the robbery.
   D whether the old man had complained a great deal.

176

1b Listen again to the conversation, then answer these questions:

1. What does his mother ask Antoine first?

2. What is her reason for asking this?

3. What is Antoine's answer?

4. What is his mother's reaction?

5. What explanation does Antoine give?

6. Where exactly did the incident described take place?

7. What does Antoine say about the old man to begin with?

8. What did the thief steal?

9. What did the old man tell Antoine?

10. What did Antoine tell the policeman he would do?

2 Listen to the cassette. You will hear a newspaper reporter interviewing a lady who has witnessed an accident. Find out why the boy was in difficulty, and how he was saved from drowning. Then say whether the statements are true or false.

1. The lady was swimming when she saw the boy in trouble.

2. The children had been playing with some old tyres.

3. The boy was shouting for help as he drifted out to sea.

4. The lady informed the lifeguard.

5. The boy was still on the airbed when the lifeguard arrived.

6. The lady gave the boy the kiss of life.

7. The ambulance arrived before the boy had been resuscitated.

3 Listen to the cassette. You will hear two boys talking. Where had the father of one of the boys been, and why? Listen again, and answer the questions.

1. How does the first boy describe the Japanese?

2. Why?

3. What does the second boy want to know?

4. What is the first boy's reaction to his friend's question?

5. What does the first robot described do?

6. What does the second do at present?

7. What do they think it might do eventually?

8. What effect does that thought have on the second boy?

4 Read this newspaper cutting, then complete the summary of what happened by filling in the gaps.

Drame devant l'hôpital

Vers 21 heures samedi soir quelques habitants du dix-neuvième arrondissement ont entendu des coups de feu. L'un d'eux s'est penché par sa fenêtre et a vu des hommes hisser à bord d'un véhicule sombre un personnage blessé.

Deux heures plus tard un homme, pistolet au poing, s'est précipité dans l'Hôpital de la Pitié pour expliquer au concierge qu'il avait laissé son ami grièvement blessé sur le trottoir et qu'il fallait agir vite. Puis l'inconnu est remonté dans un véhicule sombre qui a tout de suite disparu.

On a, en effet, trouvé un homme d'une trentaine d'années blessé par balles sur le trottoir, mais il est mort quelques minutes après dans l'entrée de l'hôpital.

The body of a man aged about . . . . . ., severely injured by . . . . . ., was placed at about . . . . . . p.m. outside a . . . . . . by the occupants of a vehicle. The man died . . . . . . later. The incident seems to have taken place in a Paris . . . . . . as . . . . . . hours earlier, local residents had heard . . . . Leaning out of his . . . . . ., one of them had seen some men putting a wounded person on a . . . . . . vehicle. On Saturday evening a stranger with a . . . . . . in his hand told the . . . . . . of the hospital that he had left a friend on the . . . . . . and that . . . . . . action was required. Then he had . . . . . . into his car and . . . .

When you read in a French newspaper about something that happened at a particular time, you often find that the Past Historic Tense is used, e.g. **il donna**, **elle sortit**.

You don't need to learn how to use this tense yourself at present, but you should learn to recognise it and to know what it means. It is always translated into English by using the simple past, i.e. he gave, she went out, they saw, etc. So you might find:

A neuf heures le directeur ouvrit la porte du magasin.

A neuf heures deux le premier client arriva.

A neuf heures cinq le téléphone sonna.

Notice that each of these events took place after the previous one.

The Past Historic is a tense that is never used in the spoken language; the Perfect Tense is used instead.

5a Read this newspaper report, then say whether the statements which follow are true or false.

Des voleurs chic

Depuis sa création en 1884 la Bijouterie Clerc qui se trouve à l'angle de la place de l'Opéra et du Boulevard des Capucines à Paris n'avait subi qu'un seul vol. Samedi dernier une deuxième attaque a eu lieu.

Deux hommes armés ont saisi les plus beaux bijoux exposés dans la vitrine la plus proche de la porte, Place de l'Opéra, sous les yeux étonnés des passants.

On se demande si c'est une coïncidence car la même vitrine avait été volée en juin 1981. Après ce premier vol les deux hommes s'étaient enfuis en moto mais samedi les voleurs ont pris le métro.

André Vincent, le directeur général de la bijouterie nous a dit qu'à 10h 30 environ il se trouvait au premier étage. Il y avait quelques clients dans le magasin qui essayaient des bagues ou qui choisissaient des parures et d'autres qui attendaient leur tour à l'atelier de réparation.

Un bel homme grand et mince aux cheveux bruns coupés court et vêtu d'un pardessus bleu marine, très bien coupé, est entré. Quand il a demandé à voir des bagues de fiançailles, une vendeuse a ouvert le cadenas qui ferme la vitrine pour en sortir des bagues.

A ce moment-là un autre homme, barbu et portant un imperméable mastic, est entré en coup de vent dans le magasin et s'est précipité dans la vitrine où il a jeté tous les bijoux à portée de main dans un grand sac. Quand une vendeuse courageuse lui a demandé ce qu'il faisait, le beau complice a sorti un revolver de sa poche et lui a recommandé de rester tranquille et de ne pas bouger.

André Vincent qui avait entendu crier la vendeuse est descendu du premier étage, tout comme il l'avait fait en 1981, pour se retrouver face au revolver de l'homme en pardessus. Cette fois personne n'a bougé parce qu'en 1981 celui qui s'était interposé s'était retrouvé à l'hôpital.

On a donc laissé les deux hommes vider la vitrine avant de partir tranquillement. On les a vus traverser la rue et disparaître dans une bouche de métro.

Quand Police-Secours est arrivée quelques instants plus tard des policiers ont essayé de rattraper les voleurs. Ils ont ramené un suspect qui portait un sac pareil à celui des gangsters mais ce n'était pas celui qu'on avait rempli de bijoux.

1. This shop has been attacked in this way twice before.

2. The raiders got away without a struggle.

3. The raid took place on Friday morning.

4. The thieves arrived on motorcycles.

5. It was too early for anybody to be in the shop.

6. The manager was on the first floor of the shop at the time.

7. A man burst into the shop and started emptying one of the showcases.

8. One of the raiders shot a sales assistant with his revolver.

9. The raiders escaped into a nearby *métro* station.

10. The police arrested the wrong man.

5b Read the report again, then write the French for these expressions:

1. a jeweller's shop;
2. a showcase;
3. a bystander;
4. a navy-blue overcoat;
5. a padlock;
6. nobody moved;
7. to empty;
8. a *métro* station entrance;
9. identical;
10. to fill.

6 Listen to the cassette. You will hear part of a radio news bulletin. There are two items of news. When you first listen, find out who escaped from where and who has recovered from what. Listen again before you answer the questions.

1. What exactly is the time of day?
2. What did the prisoners do before escaping?
3. When did they escape?
4. Have they been recaptured?
5. What two words are used to describe the recovery from brain cancer?
6. How many years of treatment had the patient had?
7. How old was she?

7a Think of everything you did this morning when you first got up; then make a list of your actions between the time you got up and the time you went to school. Remember that to make this list you will need to put all your verbs in the Perfect Tense.

7b Working with a partner, take it in turns to ask each other questions about what you did first thing this morning. Start with the question: 'A quelle heure est-ce que tu t'es levé(e) ce matin?' Then ask: 'Quand tu t'es levé(e), qu'est-ce que tu as fait ensuite?'
After the answer to that and each succeeding question, ask: 'Et puis?'

The person asking the questions should make notes on the answers given, and then check at the end to make sure the information has been taken down correctly. When you have finished, change roles.

7c Follow the same pattern as in the previous exercise, but choose a different time, asking about the evening, for instance, or another part of the morning, e.g.

A quelle heure es-tu rentré(e) hier soir?
or
A quelle heure es-tu arrivé(e) à l'école ce matin?

7d Working with a partner, practise using the Imperfect Tense in this way. Using the notes from previous exercises, ask, e.g.

Quand tu es sorti(e), que faisait ta mère?
Quand tu as fait tes devoirs, que faisaient tes frères?
Quand tu es arrivé(e), que faisaient les autres élèves?
Again make a note of each answer, check them, and change roles.

7e Using the notes you have made in the previous exercise, write ten sentences, each using a verb in the Imperfect Tense and another verb in the Perfect Tense, e.g.

Quand je suis arrivé(e) à l'école, les autres élèves travaillaient déjà.
Quand je suis rentré(e), ma sœur regardait la télévision.

8 Listen to the cassette. You will hear another news item, about a woman known as 'Mummy' Hale. Find out who she is and why she is in the news. Then listen again and answer these questions:

1. How old is 'Mummy' Hale?

2. Where does she work?

3. What is wrong with the children she works with?

4. How have they come to be like that?

5. What sort of medicine does she give them?

9 Listen to the cassette. You will hear an extract from a television news broadcast. Find out who was saved, and by whom, then listen again and answer the questions.

1. When did this happen?

2. What was the weather like at the time?

3. When the flamingo left its own lake, what was it hoping to find?

4. Where exactly did it land?

5. Who found it?

6. Where did he take it?

7. How did he treat it?

8. What did he do to make it warm?

9. What happened to it eventually?

10a Read this item from a newspaper, then write down the expressions which mean:

1. to whistle
2. a hymn;
3. the parish;
4. the congregation;
5. a service;
6. the first bars;
7. a bit of embarrassment;
8. a curate;
9. to tell someone off;
10. to prepare.

Le Vicaire qui siffle

Le Révérend David Long a eu un problème quand le pianiste qui jouait pour les offices religieux a quitté la paroisse et qu'on n'a pas pu le remplacer.

«C'est que l'assemblée semblait un peu timide quand elle devait commencer à chanter toute seule sans accompagnement musical» nous a expliqué le Révérend Long.

Celui-ci s'est donc mis à siffler les premières mesures de tous les chants religieux pour entraîner ses fidèles. La première fois on a eu un peu d'embarras mais on a vite accepté le sifflement — peut-être parce que Long a toujours été un bon siffleur.

Il nous a révélé qu'on lui avait même fait des reproches quand il était plus jeune parce qu'il sifflait en préparant son office matinal.

Sa femme Jackie nous a affirmé assez fièrement que tout le monde est d'accord pour dire que son mari siffle vraiment très bien.

10b Read the newspaper extract again, then choose the correct endings to these statements:

1. David Long whistles because
   - **A** his congregation enjoys it.
   - **B** he cannot sing.
   - **C** his church has no pianist.
   - **D** the congregation feels embarrassed.

2. He whistles
   - **A** every day.
   - **B** throughout every hymn.
   - **C** the first bars of each hymn.
   - **D** while getting ready for morning service.

11 Listen to the cassette. You will hear part of another news broadcast. Find out exactly where the fire started, and how many people had to be evacuated. Listen again, and answer these questions:

1. How many people were overcome by fumes?

2. How many of these were firemen?

3. At what time did the fire start?

4. In what sort of building?

5. Through which part of the building did the toxic smoke spread rapidly?

6. What was the final outcome of the fire?

12 Listen to the cassette. You will hear another broadcast item, dealing this time with an air crash that happened in Spain the previous day. Find out how serious it was, and what the Spanish pilots think went wrong. Listen again, and answer these questions:

1. What proves that something must be wrong with aviation in Spain?

2. How many people were killed in this crash?

3. At what time of day did it happen?

4. Where did it take place?

5. What is on the top of Mount Oïl?

6. What happened to it yesterday?

7. What kind of aeroplane was involved?

8. When were the latest navigation maps published?

13a Read this newspaper item, then complete the summary of it by filling in the gaps.

La Popularité de la France au Québec

D'après un sondage publié samedi par un quotidien de Montréal, *La Presse*, les Québécois aiment bien les Français mais ils ne connaissent que vaguement la politique française.

Il paraît que 79% des Québécois ont une opinion favorable de la France et seulement 5% une opinion défavorable. En ce qui concerne les Etats-Unis, 78% des Québécois les aiment bien mais 11% ne les aiment pas.

Par contre, si 84% des Québécois savent que Ronald Reagan est président des Etats-Unis. 37% seulement savent que François Mitterrand est président de la République Française. Mais 56% savent que Margaret Thatcher est premier ministre de la Grande Bretagne.

An . . . . published on Saturday by a Montreal . . . . . . indicates that the inhabitants of Quebec . . . . . . the French but that their knowledge of French . . . . . . is rather vague. Only 5% have an . . . . . . opinion of France whereas 11% have a similar opinion of the . . . . Most people know who is President of the United States but less than half know who is President of . . . . The . . . . of Great Britain is better known.

13b Look at the newspaper item again, then write down the French for the following expressions:

1. an inhabitant of Quebec;
2. French politics;
3. an opinion poll;
4. a daily newspaper;
5. unfavourable;

6. the United States;
7. on the other hand;
8. the President;
9. the Prime Minister;
10. Great Britain.

14a Pierre and Jeanne are neighbours, living in the same block of flats. Pierre is a professional footballer, Jeanne works part time as a solicitor. Look at this table which shows a morning's activities, then answer the questions in French.

	Pierre	Jeanne
9h	sort de la maison	
9h 30	prend le train	se lève
9h 45		prend le petit déjeuner
10h 00	descend du train	
10h 10		finit le petit déjeuner
10h 30	arrive au stade	lit son courrier
10h 55		téléphone à une amie
11h 00	match commence	
11h 10		termine sa conversation
11h 30		quitte la maison
12h 40	match se termine	
12h 45		arrive à son bureau
12h 50		voit son premier client
13h 00	déjeune au restaurant	
13h 15		son client part

1. Pendant que Jeanne dormait toujours, qu'est-ce que Pierre a fait?

2. Pendant que Jeanne se levait, qu'est-ce que Pierre a fait?

3. Pendant que Jeanne prenait son petit déjeuner, qu'est-ce que Pierre a fait?

4. Pendant que Pierre était dans le train, qu'est-ce que Jeanne a fait?

5. Pendant que Jeanne lisait son courrier, qu'est-ce que Pierre a fait?

6. Pendant que Pierre s'approchait du stade, qu'est-ce que Jeanne a fait?

7. Pendant que Jeanne parlait au téléphone, qu'est-ce qui s'est passé au stade?

8. Pendant que Jeanne était en route pour son bureau, qu'est-ce qui s'est passé au stade?

9. Pendant que Jeanne parlait à son client, qu'est-ce que Pierre a fait?

10. Pendant que Pierre déjeunait au restaurant, qu'est-ce que le client de Jeanne a fait?

14b Look again at Jeanne and Pierre's time-table, then answer these questions in French:

1. Quand Pierre est sorti de la maison, que faisait Jeanne?
2. Quand Jeanne s'est levée, que faisait Pierre?
3. Quand Pierre est descendu du train, que faisait Jeanne?
4. Quand Jeanne a fini son petit déjeuner, que faisait Pierre?
5. Quand Pierre est arrivé au stade, que faisait Jeanne?
6. Quand le match a commencé, que faisait Jeanne?
7. Quand Jeanne a quitté la maison, que faisait Pierre?
8. Quand le match s'est terminé, que faisait Jeanne?
9. Quand Pierre est arrivé au restaurant, que faisait Jeanne?
10. Quand le client de Jeanne est parti, que faisait Pierre?

15a Listen to the cassette. You will hear another extract from a news broadcast. Find out where people are going and what the two main problems are. Listen again and answer these questions:

1. What month is it?
2. What notices are the Alpine ski resorts putting up?
3. What is the snow like?
4. Why is it like this?
5. What is the weather forecast regarding snow?
6. How many extra trains are being put on?
7. How many travellers will the trains carry?
8. What will the roads be like?
9. What large operation has France-Inter launched?
10. How many local stations does Radio France have in the area?

15b Listen to the news broadcast again, then write down the French for these expressions:

1. an Alpine resort;
2. snow;
3. full;
4. wet;
5. weather forecast;
6. an extra train;
7. a traveller;
8. congested;
9. we'll say more about it;
10. on the one o'clock news.

16a Read this newspaper item, then answer the questions.

Mort de la Grande-Duchesse Charlotte de Luxembourg

Hier après-midi au château de Fischbach est morte, âgée de quatre-vingt-neuf ans, la grande-duchesse Charlotte de Luxembourg, duchesse de Nassau, princesse de Bourbon-Parme.

Cette femme bien-aimée de tous les Luxembourgeois a régné sur le Grand-Duché pendant quarante-six ans avant d'abdiquer en faveur de son fils, le grand-duc Jean, en 1964.

En principe la grande-duchesse Charlotte, si simple et élégante et passionnée par les fleurs, et qui est née au château de Berg le 23 janvier 1896, n'aurait jamais dû régner. Un héritier mâle aurait dû succéder au grand-duc Guillaume, marié à la grande-duchesse Marie-Anne de Bragance, infante du Portugal. Mais le grand-duc Guillaume n'avait pas de fils et en 1907 il déclara l'aînée de ses six filles, Marie-Adelaïde, héritière présomptive.

La grande-duchesse Charlotte, une grand-mère heureuse lors du baptême de son petit-fils, le petit prince héritier Guillaume, qu'elle tenait dans ses bras.

Le règne de la jeune princesse ne dura que sept ans parce que, en raison de ses sympathies pro-allemandes, elle dut abdiquer en faveur de sa sœur cadette, Charlotte.

Celle-ci, qui avait vingt-trois ans, venait d'épouser le prince Félix de Bourbon-Parme, descendant en ligne directe des rois de France. Quatorze mois plus tard elle donna naissance à Jean, le premier héritier présomptif à naître sur le territoire luxembourgeois et qui y règne actuellement. Charlotte eut cinq autres enfants et jusqu'à ces derniers jours elle recevait ses vingt-sept petits-enfants au château de Fischbach où elle passait le temps à faire de la lecture et du jardinage.

Au moment de son accession au trône, au lendemain de la Première Guerre Mondiale, les 366.000 habitants de son petit Etat s'interrogeaient déjà sur les mérites du système républicain.

Heureusement pour la grande-duchesse elle se fit rapidement aimée et quand on organisa un référendum huit mois plus tard, 80% des voix étaient pour elle.

Par son intelligence, son charme et son dévouement aux affaires du Grand-Duché elle gagna le respect et la reconnaissance de la population qui appréciait la prospérité et la législation sociale du pays.

Il est intéressant de constater que le Luxembourg fut parmi les premiers pays en 1919 à accorder le droit de vote aux femmes.

Lors de l'invasion du Luxembourg par l'Allemagne, le 10 mai 1940, la grande-duchesse et le gouvernement furent obligés de s'exiler d'abord en France, puis en Angleterre.

La grande-duchesse revint cinq ans plus tard pour se trouver tout aussi populaire. «Madame, nous vous aimons», lui dit spontanément le premier ministre Jean Dupong quand elle retourna le 14 avril 1945.

1. On what date did this news item appear?

2. When did the grand-duchess die?

3. How long did she reign over Luxembourg?

4. What did she do in 1964?

5. How old was she when she came to the throne?

6. Who had been on the throne immediately before her?

7. How many sisters did she have?

8. How many grandchildren did she have?

9. What happened in Luxembourg in 1919?

10. What happened in Luxembourg in 1940?

16b Look at that item again. If you were telling someone about it later, in French, how would you tell them:

1. that the grand-duchess of Luxembourg died yesterday;

2. how long she reigned over Luxembourg;

3. where she was born;

4. when she was born;

5. why Marie-Adélaïde abdicated;

6. who the grand-duchess's husband's ancestors were;

7. what her favourite pastimes were in later life;

8. how successful she was in a vote of confidence shortly after her accession;

9. what happened in 1919;

10. what she did after the German invasion in 1940?

16c Look at the newspaper extract again, and give the exact meaning of these expressions:

1. en principe;

2. en raison de;

3. ses sympathies pro-allemandes;

4. elle venait d'épouser;

5. jusqu'à ces derniers jours;

6. la lecture;

7. le lendemain de;

8. la Première Guerre Mondiale;

9. lors de l'invasion;

10. Madame, nous vous aimons.

17a Look at the incident shown in the series of pictures, and imagine you saw it happen. Write down in French exactly what the girl did. You will need to write five or six sentences, each containing a verb in the Perfect Tense.

17b Look at the incident again. Imagine that you were the boy, then write the answers to these questions in French:

1. Quand la jeune fille est sortie du cinéma, que faisais-tu?

2. Quand elle montait dans l'autobus, qu'est-ce que tu as fait?

3. Quand elle était dans l'autobus, qu'est-ce que le chien a fait?

4. Et puis qu'est-ce que tu as fait?

5. Et le chien?

6. Quand la jeune fille est descendue de l'autobus, que faisais-tu?

7. Qu'est-ce que vous avez fait ensemble ensuite?

8. Qu'est-ce que vous avez fait en vous promenant?

17c Now imagine that you are the girl, and you are writing a letter to a friend the day after this incident happened. Write the part of the letter in which you tell your friend about the incident, and say what happened afterwards. Remember to use the Perfect and Imperfect Tenses as appropriate.

Un peu de grammaire

If you want to refer to something that was already going on when something else happened, you use the Imperfect Tense. Look at this sentence:

A neuf heures le directeur a ouvert la porte du magasin.

Now imagine that at nine o'clock there were a lot of people already waiting for the shop to open; they had obviously been waiting since before nine o'clock, so you could say:

A neuf heures beaucoup de gens attendaient déjà devant le magasin.

You could also say:

Beaucoup de gens attendaient déjà devant le magasin quand le directeur a ouvert la porte.

In the same way you would say:

Je marchais dans la rue quand j'ai aperçu mon ami Jacques.

Il achetait un journal quand je l'ai vu.

Unit 15
A votre santé!

In this unit you will learn

– how to tell others how you feel

– how to ask others how they feel

– how to tell others how an accident happened

– how to ask others how an accident happened

1a Read this passage, which is an extract from a guide-book to
France written for visitors from French-speaking countries
overseas. Answer the questions on each section.

Presque tous les Français attachent une grande importance à leur
santé. Ils avalent un grand nombre de pilules chaque année et ils
passent souvent leurs vacances à faire des cures.
 Dès qu'ils ne se sentent pas bien ils vont chez le médecin, malgré le
fait qu'en France il faut payer le médecin chaque fois qu'il vous donne
une consultation. Ce n'est que plus tard que la Sécurité Sociale vous
rembourse 70 à 90% de votre argent. Vous devez aussi payer le
pharmacien quand il vous donne les médicaments que le docteur a
prescrits et c'est encore la Sécurité Sociale qui vous rembourse.

1. According to this article, what do French people do every
   year?

2. What do French people have to do when they go to see the
   doctor?

3. What does Social Security do for sick people?

4. What do you have to pay the chemist for?

1b Il y a des médecins généralistes qui soignent toutes les maladies mais beaucoup d'autres préfèrent se spécialiser comme ces médecins dont vous voyez ici les plaques.

Docteur Jacques ROBIN

Ancien externe des hôpitaux de Paris
Maladies de la peau et du cuir chevelu
Consultations de 14h. à 17h.
et sur rendez-vous

Docteur J.-P. VERNET
Acupuncture
Homéopathie
sur rendez-vous   Tél. 60-43-92

5. Why would you go and see Dr Robin?

6. When could you see him?

7. How would you arrange a consultation with Dr Vernet?

1c Si vous êtes blessé dans un accident de la route en France il vaut mieux demander qu'on vous transporte à l'hôpital plutôt qu'à une clinique où vous devrez payer cher les soins que vous recevrez. Les chauffeurs des ambulances privées qu'on trouve partout ne seront que trop heureux de vous emmener à la clinique et de vous faire payer le voyage.

8. Why is it a good idea for the victim of a road accident to ask to be taken to a hospital rather than a clinic?

9. Why might ambulance drivers prefer to take you to a clinic?

1d Read the extracts in exercises 1a, 1b and 1c again, then say exactly what is meant by these expressions:

1. presque tous les Français;

2. ils avalent un grand nombre de pilules;

3. dès qu'ils ne se sentent pas bien;

4. la Sécurité Sociale vous rembourse;

5. beaucoup d'autres;

6. sur rendez-vous;

7. si vous êtes blessé;

8. il vaut mieux demander;

9. les soins que vous recevrez;

10. ils ne seront que trop heureux.

Good health

to be well
- se porter bien
- être en bonne santé
- aller bien
- se sentir bien

to look well avoir bone mine

to recover
- guérir
- se rétablir

Illness

to be ill	être malade
to feel out of sorts	ne pas être dans son assiette
to look unwell	avoir mauvaise mine
to have a cold	être enrhumé / avoir un rhume
to have 'flu	avoir la grippe
to be feverish	avoir de la fièvre / avoir de la température
to have a pain	avoir une douleur
to cough	tousser
to sneeze	éternuer
to have a sore throat	avoir mal à la gorge
to have a headache	avoir mal à la tête
to have stomach ache	avoir mal au ventre

2a Listen to the cassette recording in which you will hear a girl talking to her father, then answer the questions.

1. What does Martine's father ask her?
2. What is her reply?
3. What does she think is wrong with her?
4. Why?
5. What does he tell her to do?
6. What does her father say he will do first?
7. What does he say he will get for her?
8. What will he do if necessary?

2b Listen to the conversation again, then write down the
expressions which mean;

1. What is the matter?   6. I have a bad headache.

2. Don't you feel well?   7. Go back to bed.

3. I don't feel well at all.   8. I'll take your temperature.

4. I must have 'flu.   9. Do you have any aspirin?

5. Do you have a temperature?   10. I'll telephone the doctor.

3 Write a list, in French, of the parts of the body that you know.
Then, working with a partner, practise conversations along
these lines:

A Say you are unwell.   **B** Ask what is wrong.

A Say you have a pain.   **B** Ask where the pain is.

A Say where the pain is.

Keep changing roles, and choose a different part of the body
each time, checking afterwards to see if you have understood
properly.

4a Listen to the cassette. You will hear a conversation between two
boys. Find out what is wrong with one of them, and what he has
done about it. Listen again and then answer the questions.

1. What does the first boy want to know first?

2. What does the second boy reply?

3. What is wrong with him?

4. When did he start to feel unwell?

5. What did the doctor do for him?

6. What doesn't the boy like about being ill?

7. What does his friend say to cheer him up?

8. What does he say he will do?

4b Listen to the conversation again, making notes on how various things are expressed. Then write down in French how you would:

1. ask a friend how he or she is;

2. say that you had had a headache for two days;

3. tell someone to be patient;

4. tell a friend not to worry;

5. ask a friend to come and see you this evening.

5 Listen to the cassette. You will hear another conversation between two friends. Find out what is wrong with one of them, and what she has done about it. Listen again and then answer the questions.

1. How does Mme Leduc think Mme Brun is looking?

2. What does Mme Brun say is wrong with her?

3. Why has she not seen the doctor?

4. What has she taken for it?

5. What does Mme Leduc tell her to do?

6. What wish does she express?

6 Imagine that you are on holiday in France, staying with a French family. One day you are feeling unwell, and you explain how you feel to the father or mother of the family you are staying with. You would need to tell them:

1. that you feel unwell;

2. where it hurts;

3. what you would like to do.

They are likely to ask you:

1. when it started;

2. whether this has happened before;

3. if you feel like eating or drinking;

4. if you have a temperature;

5. if you have taken anything for it;

6. if you would prefer to go back to bed;

7. if you would like to see the doctor.

Act out the situation with a partner, then change roles.

7a Listen to the cassette. You will hear a conversation between a young woman and her doctor. Find out why she has gone to see the doctor and what advice the doctor gives her. Listen again, and then say whether these statements are true or false:

1. The girl has caught the sun on her back.
2. She spent the previous day in the sun.
3. The sun hardly shone the previous day.
4. The doctor says that wind, water and salt are as dangerous as the sun.
5. She had spent a whole day in the sun.
6. The best time to sunbathe is between 11 and 2.

 7b Listen to the conversation again, then write down the expressions which mean:

1. Can you help me?
2. I will do my best.
3. I have had too much sun.
4. This will do you good.
5. I got burnt just the same.
6. That can happen.
7. The skin is irritated.
8. You must have spent a lot of time in the sun.
9. The day before yesterday.
10. One must be careful.

 8 Look at these instructions about sunbathing, and then make a list in English of what you should and should not do.

Pour vous protéger contre le soleil

★ Vous ne devriez pas rester au soleil entre 11h et 14h. Le soleil du matin et de la fin d'après-midi est moins dangereux.

★ Vous ne devriez pas rester couché immobile en plein soleil. L'exposition doit être progressive et non intensive, surtout si vous avez la peau claire.

★ Vous devez employer correctement les produits solaires. Demandez le conseil du pharmacien sur le type de crème qui vous convient. Renouvelez l'application toutes les trois heures en cas d'exposition prolongée et après chaque bain.

★ Tout au long des vacances vous ne devriez pas employer: les déodorants, les cosmétiques contenant de l'essence de bergamote, de citron, de lavande—les parfums et eaux de Cologne – et certains médicaments que vous indiquera votre pharmacien ou votre médecin. Pendant l'exposition solaire, ces produits entraînent la formation de taches brunes indélébiles sur la peau.

★ Pour mieux protéger votre peau, vous devriez vous rincer à l'eau douce après chaque bain de mer (sel et soleil dessèchent et fragilisent la peau).

9 Look at the advertisement and then answer the questions.

bronzer sans abîmer sa peau,
c'est normal aujourd'hui avec un bon produit solaire.

Mais bronzer et embellir sa peau en même temps, c'est ce que vous propose CLUB MEDITERRANEE de L'OREAL: parce que son filtre et sa base agissent pour vous donner une peau douce et dorée.
La GAMME SOLEIL CLUB MEDITERRANEE comprend:
– deux laits
– deux crèmes
– un lait après soleil qui refraîchit votre peau et prolonge le bronzage.

1. What does the advertisement claim the products will *not* do to your skin?

2. What does it claim the products do to your skin as well as tanning it?

3. What does the 'lait après-soleil' do?

4. What exactly does the range of products consist of?

 10 Listen to the cassette. You will hear a conversation between a man and a doctor. Find out why the man has gone to see the doctor, what his symptoms are, and what the doctor recommends. Listen again, and then answer the questions.

1. What kind of insects have stung the man?

2. When did he receive the stings?

3. Whereabouts is the swelling?

4. Where does the doctor say swelling would be dangerous?

5. When has the doctor seen stings like this before?

6. What will the cream do to help?

7. What is the man allowed to drink?

8. When must he see the doctor again?

11 Read this extract from a health booklet on insect stings and then answer the questions.

Comment soulager la douleur

Si vous n'avez qu'une simple piqûre vous ferez mieux de vous rappeler les recettes de «grand-mère»: l'eau vinaigrée.

Vous pourriez aussi utiliser un antiseptique local ou des crèmes «médicales» que votre pharmacien vous conseillera et qui peuvent aider à calmer la douleur.

N'oubliez pas que les crèmes antihistaminiques doivent toujours être employées avec la plus grande prudence.

1. What was 'granny's' remedy for an insect sting?

2. In what sort of cases is that treatment still considered all right?

3. What alternative is there?

4. How do the chemist's creams help?

5. How should anti-histamines be used?

12 Working with a partner, imagine that you are unwell and that your partner is a doctor. Work out what you think is wrong with you, what your symptoms are, and what you want to ask the doctor. The doctor should work out what he/she needs to know. Act out a situation in the doctor's surgery, then change roles and do it again.

13 Look at these instructions for three different medicines, then answer the questions.

A **Indications**
Migraines/Névralgies
Douleurs rhumatismales/Courbatures
Etats grippaux et fébriles

Posologie
1 à 4 comprimés par jour, à prendre de préférence accompagnés d'un demi-verre d'eau
Emploi réservé aux adultes

Précautions d'emploi
En cas de traitement prolongé chez le sujet atteint de dysfonctionnement rénal, ce médicament devra être utilisé sous surveillance médicale
Ne pas laisser à la portée des enfants
Ne pas dépasser les doses indiquées sans avis médical

B

INDICATIONS:

Eczémas,
dermites de contact.

Prurits,
démangeaisons,
piqûres d'insectes.

Brûlures,
érythèmes solaires.

MODE D'EMPLOI
ET POSOLOGIE:
Etendre la crème sur la région à traiter
et masser légèrement pour favoriser la
pénétration. Effectuer 2 à 3 applications
par jour.
Une éventuelle coloration jaune de la
crème après ouverture du tube n'est pas
une restriction dans l'emploi de ce
produit.

PRÉCAUTIONS D'EMPLOI:
Ne pas utiliser sur les lésions infectées
ou surinfectées.

C

Ce médicament a pour but d'améliorer votre état digestif et, en particulier, de soulager vos maux d'estomac.

Si votre médecin ou votre pharmacien vous ont donné des instructions particulières adaptées à votre cas personnel, respectez leurs consignes.
Généralement, ce médicament se prend environ 1 heure après chaque repas et/ou au moment des crises douloureuses.

Son utilisation ne doit pas vous dispenser d'une alimentation saine et régulière: en particulier, prenez le temps de manger tranquillement et, surtout, évitez de fumer ou de prendre des boissons alcoolisées longtemps après les repas ou quand vous êtes à jeun.

Si malgré ces recommandations, vos troubles persistent, n'hésitez pas à consulter votre médecin, car ce médicament ne doit pas être pris sur une période trop prolongée sans avis médical.

Au cas où vous auriez à prendre, durant la même période, un autre traitement par voie orale, il peut être préférable de respecter un intervalle entre la prise des deux médicaments.

VOTRE MEDECIN, VOTRE PHARMACIEN, CONNAISSENT LES MEDICAMENTS. N'HESITEZ PAS A LEUR DEMANDER DES PRECISIONS.

1. Which one would you use for insect bites?

2. Which one would you use if you had indigestion?

3. Which one would you use if you had 'flu?

4. Which one would you use if you had burned yourself?

5. Which one would you use if you had a headache?

6. How many of the headache pills do you need to take?

7. How often do you apply the insect-bite cream?

8. When should you take the indigestion pills?

9. What are you advised to do if your indigestion persists?

10. If you have digestive troubles, what are you advised not to do?

14 Listen to the cassette. You will hear a telephone conversation. Find out who is ringing whom and why, then answer the questions.

1. What is the full name of the boy they are talking about?

2. Why does the man think she might be worried?

3. What is her reaction?

4. What was the boy doing when the incident occurred?

5. What is the woman afraid of?

6. What does the man think she ought to do?

7. What is she going to do straight away?

15a Listen to the cassette. You will hear a conversation between a woman and a doctor. Say whether these statements are true or false.

1. The woman has cut her hand.

2. She was making an omelette at the time of the accident.

3. She spilt hot fat.

4. It doesn't hurt any more.

5. She has burned herself very badly.

6. The doctor gives her some ointment to relieve the pain.

7. She is not to eat anything hot for several days.

8. Her husband is useless at cooking.

15b Listen to the conversation again, then say exactly what these expressions mean:

1. Comment l'accident s'est-il produit?

2. La poêle a pris feu.

3. Vous avez très mal?

4. Ça va un peu mieux maintenant.

5. Vous n'aurez plus mal.

6. Faites attention.

16a Read this advertisement for health resorts, then answer the
questions.

VOTRE « FORME » EN PRATIQUE

DES FORCES NEUVES A EVIAN :
Cure biologique, soins douceur, complexe sportif et gastronomie diététique. Mieux-vivre et tradition : un cocktail très réussi.

A ÉVIAN

Royal Hôtel, 75500 Evian-les-Bains. Tél. : (50) 75.14.00.
Il est préférable d'arriver le dimanche. Accueil et information à 19 heures.
− Forfait diététique (7 jours) : de 3 290 F à 4 690 F ;
− Forfait Mieux-Vivre (6 jours) : de 4 160 F à 5 560 F ;
− Super-forfait diététique et Mieux-Vivre (1 semaine) : de 4 580 F à 5 980 F ;
− Cure Biologique : en supplément des tarifs de l'hôtel. A partir de 2 500 F. Cer-

tains examens sont pris en charge par la Sécurité sociale.

A SAINT-MALO

Hôtel des Thermes Marins, Grande plage, 35401 Saint-Malo. Tél. : (99) 56.02.56.
− Tarif journalier de la cure : du 6 au 30 avril 1984, de 156 F à 210 F ; à partir du 1er mai : de 167 F à 223 F ;
− Tarif hôtel (pension) : février-mars, de 250 F à 390 F pour 1 pers., de 440 F à 560 F pour 2 pers. ; avril à juin, de

320 F à 440 F pour 1 pers., de 490 F à 630 F pour 2 pers.

EN ITALIE

Centre Mességué, Villa Soligo, 31010 Soligo-Trévise. Tél. : 0438/83572 ou 83559.
Secrétariat en France, Immeuble Le Cécil, 7, avenue Thiers, 06000 Nice. Tél. : (93) 87.21.35.
− Forfait de 13 jours : tout compris : 9 500 FF.
Arrivée le dimanche obligatoire car la cure débute le lundi. A partir de juillet, check-up complet gratuit et électrocardiogramme.

EN SUISSE

Hôtel du Golf, 3963 Crans-Montana. Tél. : 027.41.23.95.
− Forfait pension complète pour 13 jours : de 8 000 FF à 14 000 FF, − selon la saison et la catégorie de la chambre − électrocardiogramme et check-up compris.
Les soins et les examens peuvent être pris en charge par la Sécurité sociale s'il y a accord préalable.

PHOTO J. R. BESSE

1. What kind of 'cure' is offered at Evian?

2. On what day should patients arrive?

3. At Saint-Malo, what is the daily cost of treatment from 1 May onwards?

4. When are the hotel prices at Saint-Malo lowest?

5. In Italy, what do you get for about 9500 francs?

6. What is free from July onwards?

7. In Switzerland, what accounts for the price differences?

8. Who will pay for treatments and examinations if agreement is reached beforehand?

201

16b Imagine that you want to go to Saint-Malo. Write a letter to the hotel mentioned in the advertisement, saying when you would like to go and for how long, how many people will be going, and that you would like to book a 'cure' as well.

17 Read these two extracts from an article in which a doctor talks about commonly held beliefs concerning health, then answer the questions.

L'obésité

Si les enfants et les adolescents mangent ou boivent trop, cela n'a pas d'importance, car ils ont besoin de plus de calories que les adultes et, en tout cas, tout finit par rentrer dans l'ordre.

Erreur! Il faut enseigner la diététique dès l'enfance, parce que les mauvaises habitudes acquises dans l'enfance sont une des plus grandes causes de l'obésité rebelle qui afflige tant d'aultes.

L'eau

Une des plus vieilles idées reçues est celle qui enseigne qu'en buvant beaucoup d'eau on fait dilater l'estomac.

Erreur! Pourvu qu'on la boive lentement l'eau ne cause pas une dilation de l'estomac. On se porte très bien si on en boit un litre et demi par jour, c'est-à-dire environ un verre par heure. N'oublions pas qu'à partir de la cinquantaine on tend à moins avoir soif.

1. Why do many people believe that children and adolescents can over-eat without coming to any harm?
2. Why is this belief incorrect?
3. What do many people believe is caused by drinking a great deal of water?
4. How should water be drunk?
5. How much water should be drunk every day to remain in good health?
6. At what age do people begin to feel less thirsty?

18 Imagine that you have been ill, and have been unable to write to your French pen-friend for a while. Write apologising for this, and tell your friend what was wrong with you, what your symptoms were, when you saw the doctor, what the doctor said, what you had to do, how long you had to stay in bed, when you started to feel better, how you are feeling now, and when you can go back to school.

19a Look at the series of pictures, and imagine you saw this incident happen last week. Working with a partner, tell your partner in French what you saw. Your partner may ask questions about anything that is unclear or that you have missed out. Then change roles, with your partner telling you about the incident.

 19b Look at the series of pictures again, and imagine that you are either the boy or the girl who fetched the doctor. A few days later you write to a French friend. Write the part of the letter in which you tell your friend about this incident.

Un peu de grammaire

If you are ill, or in pain, a doctor is likely to ask you how long you have been feeling like that. The answer to such a question in French is

Depuis trois heures.

Depuis deux jours.
or
Depuis un mois.

– depending on the circumstances.

Now, since you are still suffering from whatever it is at the time of speaking to the doctor, you might say, e.g.

J'ai mal à la tête.

Je suis enrhumée.
or
Je ne suis pas dans mon assiette.

If you want to say both how you are feeling now and how long you have been feeling like that, you can combine the two in one sentence, like this:

J'ai mal à la tête depuis trois heures.

Je suis enrhumée depuis deux jours.

Je ne suis pas dans mon assiette depuis un mois.

Notice that, although in English we would say 'I *have had* a headache for three hours', using a past tense, in French you use the Present Tense, the idea being that you still have a headache now, and you simply add **depuis trois heures** to indicate when it started.